Tickets to Paradise

A History of Key West Travel and Its Advertising

1912-1975

Jennifer Patterson Lorenzetti

Copyright © 2017 Jennifer Patterson Lorenzetti

Published by Hilltop Communications

All rights reserved.

ISBN: 0692943544
ISBN-13: 978-0692943540

DEDICATION

To my parents, Michael A. and Janice C. Patterson, who have always encouraged my dreams – especially when they are dreams of palm trees and balmy sea breezes.

To my husband, Daniel Lorenzetti, who, on our honeymoon, took me down a quiet, historic side street in Key West and thus started two love affairs that would last a lifetime.

And, to everyone who is reading this book with their toes in the sand, a drink in their hand, and a curiosity about the southernmost city. May you explore, may you learn, and may you always keep a bit of Key West with you.

ACKNOWLEDGEMENTS

I would like to thank the following for their assistance with this work:

The Florida Keys Public Library, with special thanks to Tom Hambright
The Key West Art and Historical Society
Casa Marina Resort

I would also like to thank the Hemingway Society and conference chair Raul Villarreal, for allowing me to debut Chapter 3 at the 2017 Hemingway Between Key West and Cuba conference.

Additionally, I would like to thank my husband, Daniel, for technical assistance throughout the layout process and beyond.

My thanks go to all these experts; any errors are mine alone.

JPL
2017

TABLE OF CONTENTS

ACKNOWLEDGEMENTS IV

TABLE OF FIGURES 1

PROLOGUE 3

CHAPTER ONE: FLAGLER'S FOLLY 7
- Connections South 8
- Advertising Paradise 9
- Preparing for Tourism 19

CHAPTER 2: THE HOUSE BY THE SEA 21
- The House by the Sea 23
- Tourism before the Great Depression 30
- The Power of Celebrity Endorsement 33
- The Luxury of Pan Am 34

CHAPTER 3: OBSERVING THE HEMINGWAYS 37
- FERA and the Great Depression 37
- Invasions of Privacy 40
- The Reinvention of the Island 43
- The Labor Day Hurricane 50
- the United States – like the robust car culture that would develop in the 20th century. 53
- "See the U.S.A...." 53
- Road's End 54

CHAPTER 4: INTERMEZZO 57
- World War II 59
- Harry Truman and the Little White House 61
- The Cuban Missile Crisis 62

CHAPTER 5: FAMILY FUN 65
- Rubbing Elbows 71
- Vintage Selfies: The Postcard as Travel Marketing 72

CHAPTER 6: BEFORE MARGARITAVILLE 79
- Marketing to the Conchs 80
- The Mallory Square Sunset Celebration 83
- Air Sunshine 84

EPILOGUE 87

Jennifer Patterson Lorenzetti

TABLE OF FIGURES

Figure 1: 1913 Arts and Crafts advertisement for Florida East Coast Railway (Available under Wikimedia Commons.) 11

Figure 2: Bifold brochure showing Key West as the gateway to the Caribbean, Central America, and South America. (Courtesy Florida Keys Public Library.) 13

Figure 3: Bifold brochure for Key West and Monroe County, highlighting the "frost free" climate. (Available under Creative Commons with attribution: Florida Keys Public Library MM00030826.) 15

Figure 4: A brochure for the Florida East Coast Railway showing a melding of both Arts and Crafts and Art Nouveau advertising styles. (Available under Creative Commons with attribution: Florida Keys Public Library MM00030988.) 18

Figure 5: A postcard for the Over Sea Hotel, likely intended as an intermediate stop for travelers taking the railroad to Key West and sea transportation further south. (Available under Creative Commons with attribution: Florida Keys Public Library MM00039032x.) 22

Figure 6: Singer Rudy Vallee (R) at the Casa Marina from the Jeff Broadhead Collection at the Florida Keys Public Library. (Available under Creative Commons with attribution: Florida Keys Public Library MM00014027x.) ... 27

Figure 7: 907 Whitehead Street, originally owned by Asa Tift and later by Ernest Hemingway. From the Scott DeWolfe Collection at the Florida Keys Public Library.(Available under Creative Commons with attribution: Florida Keys Public Library MM00042282x.) 41

Figure 8: Postcard showing arrival and unloading of a turtle boat, likely either at the future site of the Key West Aquarium or at the Turtle Kraals, from the Florida Keys Public Library. (Available under Creative Commons with attribution: Florida Keys Public Library MM00012833.) 43

Figure 9: Construction of Key West Aquarium circa 1935. (Available under Creative Commons with attribution: Florida Keys Public Library MM00088834x.) 44

Figure 10: Key West Aquarium circa 1950. (Available under Creative Commons with attribution: Florida Keys Public Library MM00039510x.) 45

Figure 11: Reproduction of an Alfred D. Crimi mural for the Key West Aquarium, 1998. (Available under Creative Commons with attribution: Florida Keys Public Library MM00033840x.) 47

FIGURE 12: SCREENCAP OF CHEVROLET NEWSREEL SHOWING THE ROAD BED OF WHAT WOULD BECOME U.S. 1 WITH A 1935 CHEVY HANDLING THE BOUNCE-INDUCING TERRAIN. FROM CHEVROLET LEADER NEWS, VOL. 1, NO. 2, 1935. (AUTHOR'S COLLECTION.) 53

FIGURE 13: ALL ROADS END AT KEY WEST FLORIDA, ACCORDING TO THIS 1930S BROCHURE. (AVAILABLE UNDER CREATIVE COMMONS WITH ATTRIBUTION: FLORIDA KEYS PUBLIC LIBRARY MM41339-13X.) 56

FIGURE 14: TWO MEN STAND ATOP WEST MARTELLO OBSERVING THE FLEET IN THE HARBOR WITH FORT TAYLOR IN THE DISTANCE. (AVAILABLE UNDER CREATIVE COMMONS WITH ATTRIBUTION: FLORIDA KEYS PUBLIC LIBRARY MM00041084X.) 58

FIGURE 15: CONCERTINA WIRE ON SMATHERS BEACH DURING THE CUBAN MISSILE CRISIS, 1962. (AVAILABLE UNDER CREATIVE COMMONS WITH ATTRIBUTION: FLORIDA KEYS PUBLIC LIBRARY MM00046461X.) 63

FIGURE 16: U.S. ROUTE 1 SIGN ON NORTH ROOSEVELT BOULEVARD C. 1950. (AVAILABLE UNDER CREATIVE COMMONS WITH ATTRIBUTION: FLORIDA KEYS PUBLIC LIBRARY MM00004977X.) 69

FIGURE 17: POSTCARD OF THE OCEAN VIEW HOTEL COTTAGES, C. 1950. (AVAILABLE UNDER CREATIVE COMMONS WITH ATTRIBUTION: FLORIDA KEYS PUBLIC LIBRARY MM00013313X.) 72

FIGURE 18: SUN AND SAND CLUB POSTCARD, 1435 SIMONTON STREET. (AVAILABLE UNDER CREATIVE COMMONS WITH ATTRIBUTION: FLORIDA KEYS PUBLIC LIBRARY MM00032654.) 74

FIGURE 19: SANTA MARIA POSTCARD, 1401 SIMONTON STREET. (AVAILABLE UNDER CREATIVE COMMONS WITH ATTRIBUTION: FLORIDA KEYS PUBLIC LIBRARY MM00032658.) 75

FIGURE 20: POSTCARD OF CACTUS TERRACE, 725 TRUMAN AVENUE. (AVAILABLE UNDER CREATIVE COMMONS WITH ATTRIBUTION: FLORIDA KEYS PUBLIC LIBRARY MM00032650.) 76

FIGURE 21: A POSTCARD OF PRESIDENT EISENHOWER ON TRUMAN AVENUE. (AVAILABLE UNDER CREATIVE COMMONS WITH ATTRIBUTION: FLORIDA KEYS LIBRARY MM00013524X.) 77

PROLOGUE
"Before the railroad claimed the southernmost frontier"[1]

Drive south on Interstate 75, and you know within seconds of entering Florida that this state is serious about its tourism. The first travelers' information center you encounter is not your average empty state-run visitor's center. Instead, this one is staffed by a complement of almost aggressively enthusiastic ambassadors, ready to connect everyone who enters with all they will need to enjoy their stay. Barely two miles from the Georgia-Florida border, travelers can rent a condo, book a hotel, buy Disney World tickets, and learn about other attractions, all while they stretch their car-weary legs and grab a snack from the vending machine.

The experience is similar up and down the state. No opportunity to advertise to Florida's visitors is missed, from the first flamingo-decorated billboard near the state line all the way to Key West at the southernmost tip. Billboards march down the highway shoulders like an army; airports are dotted with the latest digital signage; information racks are stuffed with brochures; and magazines are filled with print ads. Floridians market to state outsiders like their lives depend on it. And, with tourism being Florida's largest business (with an economic impact of $109 billion in 2016[2]), livelihoods do depend on this marketing.

But before the turn of the 20th century, this was not the case, especially for tiny Key West. Located at the end of a chain of coral reef islands known as the Florida Keys, Key West has always required a bit of gumption and effort to visit.

Although the island today is thought of as a small town that is dwarfed by the city of Miami some 120 miles to the north, the reverse was originally true. In the 1800s, when the fastest mode of transportation on the planet moved not on land but on the sea, Key West was prized for its strategic maritime value, both from its location near Cuba, the Bahamas, and New Orleans, and from its position in the Gulf Stream that runs up the east coast from the Straits of Florida. Fast sailing made this intermediate port a location of value to the military and, quickly, to a variety of industries. By 1890, Key West's port was ranked the thirteenth busiest in the United States.[3]

The military took advantage of Key West's position as the southernmost point of U.S. land to establish defenses against piracy, a very real threat to those using the Straits of Florida for a shipping channel. Ever-prepared, the navy also saw Key West as an ideal place to position forts to guard against attacks by sea from the south. These preparations fortunately turned out to be unnecessary, and Fort Zachary Taylor, itself now a tourist attraction, boasts of never having seen the elephant – never being involved in battle.

The island's primary non-military industries were fabulously lucrative, but they required hard work. The wrecking and salvage industry – watching for shipwrecks on the treacherous coral reefs; rescuing the passengers, crew, and cargo; and, often, selling the cargo back to the rescuees once all were safely aground – called for long nights, skillful seamanship, and a good mind for business. This industry built the Key West Lighthouse and the beautiful two-story home with wraparound porches situated on Whitehead Street and owned by salvage magnate Asa Tift, who valued its location across from the lighthouse that allowed him to get early notification of a wreck and a potential cargo to salvage. Tourists flock to Tift's house today, but they generally know only of the house's most famous resident, Ernest Hemingway, who lived there with second wife Pauline during the Great Depression.

Key West's other major pre-railroad industries included sponging, turtling, salt-production, and cigar manufacturing. The first three of these are harvesting jobs, involving a great deal of physical effort and not a small bit of physical risk while working in the oppressive heat and humidity of the Key West docks. Taking advantage of Key West's rich natural resources, these industries supplied turtle meat, natural sponges, and sea salt to the world.

The last industry, made possible by revolution in Cuba that caused cigar manufacturers to relocate 90 miles north to Key West, involved long days in steamy pre-air conditioning factories, where Cuban workers would sit at long benches and roll cigars by hand while a lector read newspapers and books aloud for their entertainment. At night, the cigar rollers would return to homes known as "conch houses," a type of shotgun shack still seen throughout the island.

By the end of the 19th century, these industries had made Key West both the richest city in Florida and the largest, with almost 10,000 residents. This large city of hard-working affluence would hold its position as America's gem of the Caribbean until the late 1920s.

But the uniting feature of all of Key West's first industries was the insularity of their populations. Whether one was a sponger, a cigar roller, a salvage magnate, or a naval officer, working in Key West meant a time-intensive relocation by boat to the little island. Anything the residents wanted would have to be provided locally, and the island quickly grew a variety of services still reflected in building and street names: churches, schools, a marine hospital, and even a poor house.

The Conchs (the local name for a resident that continues on in modern times) understood the isolated nature of their existence as well. For example, legend has it that refrigeration was such a late arrival to the sub-tropical city that the iconic key lime pie was invented as a way to preserve the milk that would otherwise rapidly spoil. The island's sense of frontier isolation would later bring writers, musicians, and other misfits to its shores, seeking the quiet and safety from the mainland world that would allow them to live their own lives in peace.

Ships may come and go from its busy port, but Key West had very little in the way of a truly transient population before the 20th century. This all changed when a man named Henry Morrison Flagler decided, like many Ohio residents after him would do, that he would much rather be in Florida during the winter.

CHAPTER ONE: FLAGLER'S FOLLY
The Florida East Coast Railway and the Key West Extension

Think of the heroes of the Industrial Revolution, and certain names come immediately to mind: Andrew Carnegie, John D. Rockefeller, John Jacob Astor III. But when school children learn about these wealthy men who balanced philanthropy with cutthroat business practices at the dawn of the 20th century, they typically don't learn the story of Henry Morrison Flagler. The omission is a notable gap in the story of building the United States during the time that engineering prowess and control over raw materials gave some the opportunity to literally craft their landscape. This was the era of the construction of the Brooklyn Bridge, the spread of Carnegie libraries across the nation's college campuses, and the meeting of east and west railroad routes at that famous gold spike. What Flagler would accomplish with the Florida East Coast Railway would have echoes of all these projects.

Henry M. Flagler was born in upstate New York but relocated to Ohio as a young man, where he worked in the Harkness family store. Flagler would marry one of the Harkness daughters, Mary. Mary's untimely death would help shape Flagler's later desire for an easier route south.

However, it is the meeting of Flagler and John D. Rockefeller that can be thought of as the true beginning of the quest to connect

Key West with the mainland. Flagler and Rockefeller met while working in the grain and salt businesses, and in 1867, they formed the partnership of Rockefeller, Andrews, and Flagler. When the firm was incorporated in 1869, it was renamed the Standard Oil Company. Although the Rockefeller name is most typically associated with Standard Oil, Rockefeller himself laid credit for the firm with Flagler. In a 1910 interview about the origins of Standard Oil, Rockefeller told *Everybody's Magazine*, "No sir, I wish I had the brains to think of it. It came about because of Henry M. Flagler."[4] Standard Oil may have given Rockefeller his reputation, but it gave Flagler the resources to move to his next project.

Flagler spent his life devising solutions to problems through knowledge and engineering. His first wife, Mary, suffered from consumption, a catch-all term for pulmonary disease, and Flagler noted that she improved upon spending the winter in Jacksonville. However, the return to the cold winters of Ohio did not allow the improvement to continue, and she died in 1881. Perhaps remembering the ill effect of this wintertime cold, Flagler moved to St. Augustine with his second wife, Ida, where he would conceive and refine his dream to connect the mainland to Key West, with a string of hotels dotting the line.

Connections South

The notion of building a railroad to Key West did not originate with Flagler. Indeed, the first newspaper article mentioning the concept was printed in 1831. Just four decades later, the Great Southern Railway was incorporated, with the description of the planned lines noting "This railroad is designed to connect the entire railway system of the United States with Cuba, the…West Indies…and South America.…[It] runs…due south to Key West."[5]

The Great Southern Railway did not ultimately claim the route to Key West, but Flagler also almost passed up the southernmost prize. Flagler's initial plans called for the route to end at Cape Sable, located at the southwest tip of the mainland of Florida. Cape Sable, like Key West, would have served as a deep water port that ships could use for restocking and refueling before heading west to New Orleans or south to the Caribbean or to Central or South America. However, a railroad engineer squashed this dream by pointing out the logistical difficulties of constructing a heavy railroad across the swampy territory at Florida's tip. "Mr. Flagler, there is not enough fill on the face of the earth to build a railroad across the Everglades," he reportedly said.[6] Undeterred for long, Flagler ordered a survey to learn more about building a railroad to Key West

Reaching Key West would not be a simple task, however. The most challenging part of the construction would involve bridging the seven mile gap between Knight's Key and Bahia Honda. Constructing this stretch of railway would take all of the engineering knowledge of the time, requiring builders to create a span of bridge sitting on an ocean floor under water some 24 feet deep at low tide in some spots. But when this stretch of the Over-Sea Railway was complete, it became the iconic visual representation of the Florida East Coast Railway. Depictions of this span of bridge, with an engine steaming south, would decorate Florida East Coast marketing collateral until its destruction in the hurricane of 1935.

By 1911, Henry Flagler was in ill health, and the railroad executives ordered an increase in effort so that Flagler would get to see his great creation reach Key West. On January 22, 1912, the first official train would pull into Key West station, bearing the aged Flagler. Lore holds that he listened to the commotion around him, including a children's choir assembled in his honor, and proclaimed, "I cannot see the children, but I can hear them singing." Flagler would pass away on May 20, 1913.

Advertising Paradise

The Florida East Coast Railway would advertise its eventual terminus in Key West before the tracks reached the southernmost island. Even before Flagler's train pulled into Key West in 1912, the advertising showed the messaging that would characterize the early years of the Florida East Coast Railway. "The East Coast of Florida is Paradise Regained," proclaims the cover of a 1900 publication by

Florida East Coast. The Florida East Coast Steamship Co. routes, which included a route to Nassau, a direct route to Havana, and a route to Havana via Key West, showed the value of reaching the southernmost key before the railroad was even in place.[7]

In a 1904 booklet[8], the cover illustration features a brick gateway, likely meant to represent the city gates of St. Augustine, introducing the reader to a path flanked by palm trees leading toward a climate of sunshine and happiness. Encased within a strong but simple border and surmounted by a prominent "Florida East Coast" headline-cum-product-name, both techniques characteristic of the Arts and Crafts movement, the illustration serves to introduce the primary message of the ad. "The East Coast of Florida is Paradise Regained," is printed across the bottom of the path, a repetition of the company's tagline.

Also characteristic of the era is an unapologetic use of people of color in positions of service to indicate luxury and status to the primary target market. Joining the brick pillars in flanking the path to paradise are two dark-skinned men in servant's attire, each holding a piece of luggage and gesturing welcomingly to the reader of the brochure. These porters are clearly here to serve, not to guide, as they gesture the reader forward into the wilderness of palm trees, bisected only by a simple dirt path. Although jarring to the modern eye, this type of depiction was used to advertise everything from luxury goods to Cream of Wheat, and it reflected both a diminishing use of domestic "help" by all but the most affluent classes and the country's conflicting emotions about race.

By the first decades of the 20th century, domestic help, long the first step on the economic ladder for former slaves and recent immigrants, was beginning to decline in use. Housewives were now expected to manage a middle class household on their own with only the barest of assistance, thanks in part to industrial efficiency movements that moved from the factory to the home. The modern work triangle, which placed refrigerator (or ice box), stove, and sink in a triangular pattern that decreased steps made cooking an easier

Figure 1: 1913 Arts and Crafts advertisement for Florida East Coast Railway. (Available under Wikimedia Commons.)

task, while modern appliances like the electric refrigerator retrofit, the electric toaster, and the light bulb were beginning to make households easier to maintain. New convenience foods, like Campbell's condensed soups, trumpeted their role in making an elegant meal that suggested an alternative to the now-non-existent hired cook.[9] And advertising for luxuries, which the Florida East Coast Railway certainly was, featured stereotypical servants that indicated the level of affluence to which these services catered. The ad mentioned is an example of this.

A 1913 advertisement[10] for the new Florida East Coast Railway emphasizes the style of the period as well as the primary sales arguments for the railroad. The ad is an excellent example of the Arts and Crafts style of advertising.

A graphic style popularized by William Morris and others, the advertising style relies on simple architectural borders, prominent headlines or product name treatments, realistic illustrations, and a great deal of body copy.

In this ad, a stylized group of palm tree fronds highlights the word "Florida" at the top of the piece, with "East Coast" floating just below in a banner. A strong but simple border encloses several paragraphs of copy, while the arches of the railroad trestle in a line drawing at the bottom provide the architectural element so often seen in this style. This particular view of the seven-mile long bridge that would serve as the architectural and engineering showpiece of the entire Key West extension was featured widely on brochures, playing cards, railroad-issue china, and even the logo of the Key West Extension of the entire Florida East Coast Railway.

What's notable, however, is the dual argument made to attract both tourists and business to use the railroad. "Every Day a June Day, Full of Sunshine" the headline reads, adding "Where Winter Exists in Memory Only." The copy highlights the many activities that might draw visitors to Florida, a list that would be familiar today: golf, tennis, surf bathing (swimming), horseback riding, motoring (pleasure driving), yachting, rowing, fishing, and hunting. The middle section of the ad names several resorts and hotels located between St. Augustine and Key West.

The final section of the ad speaks to the businessman, announcing "New Route to the Panama Canal." Body copy proclaims, "The Overseas Railroad to Key West, one of the marvels of the 20th Century, has opened up a new and shorter route to Uncle Sam's latest and greatest enterprise, the Panama Canal, connecting at Key West via palatial steamers, sailing twice monthly for Colon, Panama." Clearly, Key West was being marketed as a prime location

Figure 2: Bifold brochure showing Key West as the gateway to the Caribbean, Central America, and South America. (Courtesy Florida Keys Public Library.)

for business, one that it had already held throughout its history.

The ad could not appeal to the businessman alone. Because a business centered in Key West did not allow for easy back and forth to a home base further north, even with the coming of the railroad, the businessman was likely to bring his family on a long-term temporary or permanent basis. This ad skillfully bridges that gap, mentioning enticements that would appeal to the family while also playing up the strategic business aspects.

This business-centered approach to advertising would continue into the coming era of luxury destination tourism. In a brochure printed circa 1920s[11] advertising Key West and Monroe County, the island is a literal backdrop to the locations further south to which it gives easy access. Spreading across the front and back covers of the brochure is an illustration of the island of Key West before much filling and terraforming had taken place, leaving viewers with a quaint picture of the island minus the northeast half that it would grow throughout the twentieth century.

Houses cluster in the southernmost part of the island now called Old Town, while steamships and sailboats cruise to and from the docks. The areas of the island now known as Midtown and New Town are still narrow strips of land bordering the salt flats, including the site of the current airport. The Florida East Coast Railway cruises into the city via dramatic bridges that disappear into the ocean to the northeast.

The most prominent feature of the brochure, however, is not Key West but a stunning alabaster gate that proclaims "Gateway to Cuba, West Indies, Panama Canal, Central America, and South America." Key West was a connector, a hub, a central point for travel, but it was not yet always positioned as a destination of its own. The idea of Key West as an island at the end of the world was still some decades away; this Key West was firmly embedded in its world, both isolated and at the same time at the heart of it all.

Advertising of Key West in the first two decades of the 20th century nearly always took this approach. While today's visitors think of the island as a destination of its own, early marketing positioned the little key as attractive to two populations. Primarily, Key West still saw itself as a hub for business; the island boasted the highest per capita wealth in the United States as recently as 1860, and this affluence would continue until the Great Depression. The island became home to wealthy businessmen and workers in the industries that supported them, while families that accompanied these men built the infrastructure of the island. Advertising needed to address both

Figure 3: Bifold brochure for Key West and Monroe County, highlighting the "frost free" climate. (Available under Creative Commons with attribution: Florida Keys Public Library MM00030826.)

populations, with information about the benefits of climate and the availability of resources and activities to sweeten the deal for a family being asked to abandoned their lives, perhaps in a more sophisticated city, for a business hub that was still very much a frontier town.

Marketing collateral aimed at marketing Key West itself took a very basic approach to introducing the charms of the city, as would befit early marketing efforts. In an undated but likely pre-1920 brochure aimed at introducing Key West and Monroe County, Florida, to the reader, we see a classic example of the preemptive claim in advertising[12].

The preemptive claim is a strategy that takes a characteristic of the entire product category and uses it to promote one specific brand or option. An example of this is early advertising for Schlitz beer, which proclaimed that their bottles were "washed with live steam." The fact that nearly all bottlers sterilized their bottles with steam was preempted by Schlitz, removing this argument as an option for any other brand of beer.[13] The preemptive claim is still in use today, used mostly when advertising a new product that wants to take the attributes of an entire category of goods or services and ascribe those to its own brand.

In this brochure, the weather in Key West takes center stage. While it is true that there are certain attributes of Key West weather that are unique to that city – "The southernmost and only FROST-FREE city in the United States," the subhead screams – warm winter weather is hardly exclusive to one small island. Nonetheless, the preemptive claim takes center stage with the body copy, which appears both front and back on the document: "A climate unsurpassed; never too hot, never too cold. Destined by Nature to be the Riviera of America. The ideal spot for winter homes. Every day brings new opportunities for life out of doors." The point is driven home with a realistic Arts and Crafts style illustration that depicts a palm tree, a sail boat, a fish leaping upward for pursuit by a sport fisherman, and, of course, Flagler's railroad as it steams over sea on a bridge.

There is relatively little existing advertising for Key West specifically that was created during the first two decades of the century, but that which does exist is notable both for its marketing strategy and for the design style that it typically uses to advance its message. As noted, most of the existing advertising would be considered Arts and Crafts style, typically a solid, workmanlike style used for everyday items like soap and food products. The Arts and Crafts style leaves plenty of room for body copy, which is typically used to make a sales argument for the superiority of one brand over another or to educate the reader about how to purchase the item sold.

The Florida East Coast Railway was clearly a luxury service, targeting the affluent businessman and his family. One might expect, then, that the railway would opt to use the Art Nouveau style of advertising also popular during this period. The Art Nouveau style of advertising is characterized by complex illustrations featuring detailed depiction of organic elements, like vines, flowers, or flowing hair, and it typically promoted only the product or company name without much in the way of additional body copy. The Art Nouveau style sold a fantasy of a way of life to the consumer with the implicit message that to buy a certain product was to adopt the cultural markers of a certain way of living.

While one might expect the Florida East Coast Railway to use this approach, the use of the Arts and Crafts style tells us a great deal about how the line saw itself and its purpose. Fundamentally, then, the Florida East Coast Railway saw itself not as a vehicle for tourism but as a method of transportation for business. The advertising of this time is notable for its outward-facing approach; Key West was not an idyllic destination in and of itself, but rather a base of operations from which to access and utilize the resources and strategic power of the area. Advertising of Key West in the first two decades of the 20th century nearly always took this approach.

Even the announcement of the opening of the Key West Extension[14], surely the ideal opportunity for selling the railway as luxury, married both Art Nouveau and Arts and Crafts style for a feel that is much more a precursor of the Art Deco style that would dominate the 1920s. Created in shades of ocean blue and mango, the announcement maintains the strict and simple Arts and Crafts borders while allowing an artistic and more abstract depiction of palm trees, pineapples, and tropical flowers to grace the outside edge. A central coat of arms hints at the upscale nature of the railroad. It is an interesting departure from the usual "reason why" strategy and straight-forward approach that characterized much of the advertising of the period.

Businesses opting for a base in Key West were likely considering

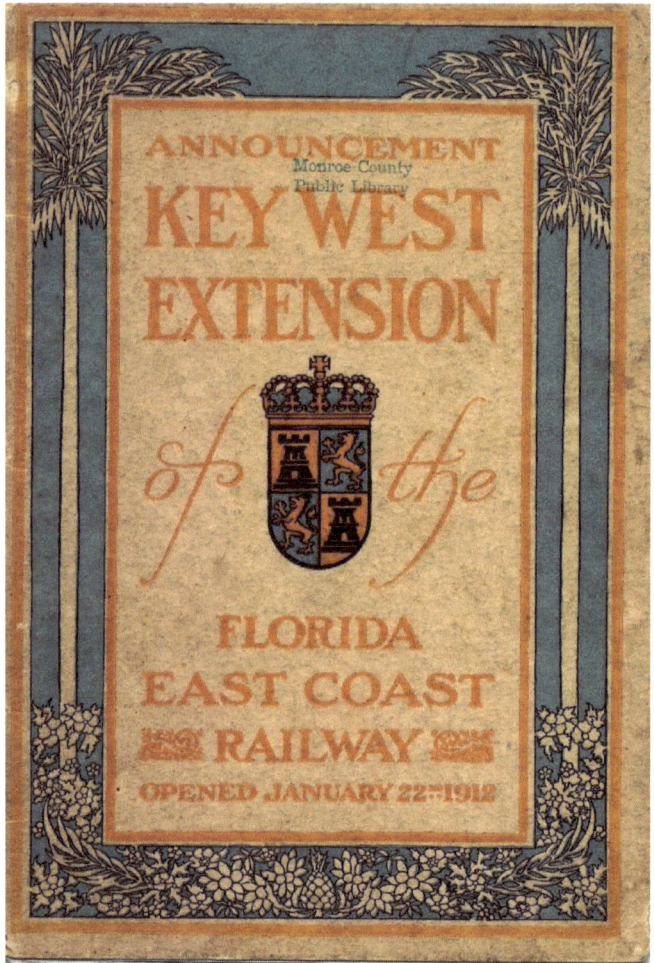

Figure 4: A brochure for the Florida East Coast Railway showing a melding of both Arts and Crafts and Art Nouveau advertising styles. (Available under Creative Commons with attribution: Florida Keys Public Library MM00030988.)

the efficiency of using this port as a midpoint in a shipping route or as a base of operations from which to access Central and South America without leaving the United States. Key West was competing with other major cities like New Orleans for business, and the advertising made this argument. Choosing Key West, then, was more a need than a luxury, and it is natural that the Florida East Coast Railway would use a sales argument-based style to advertise itself.

As for the luxury hotels along the way and the perpetual June-like climate (likely an overstatement that anyone spending August in Key West would refute), these were benefits that made conducting business and relocating a family more palatable. They were not yet the prime attraction that would bring people to the island with thoughts of leaving business behind rather than conducting it.

Preparing for Tourism

The arrival of the railroad meant Key West was poised to become a vacation destination for the affluent traveler. The first tourist attraction was, of course, the weather, and marketing materials trumpeted the warm temperatures of America's only frost free zone, along with some of the luxury hotels to be found along the journey.

The Florida East Coast Railway has often been called "Flagler's Folly," with the lure of alliteration too strong to resist merely for accuracy. In truth, the building of a railroad reaching the southernmost point in the U.S. is one of the 20th century's great triumphs of engineering and business acumen, and it opened Key West as a realistically reachable destination for the rest of the country. Never again would Key West be primarily a base of operations from which to reach outward and southward; from this point forward, Key West would be a desirable endpoint all its own. And a city reached by an epic train journey deserved a stunning resort for its visitors. It would find that destination resort in the Casa Marina.

Jennifer Patterson Lorenzetti

CHAPTER 2: THE HOUSE BY THE SEA
Casa Marina and the Affluent 1920s

Although he will be remembered as a railroad magnate, Henry Flagler was also the king of luxury hotels at the turn of the twentieth century. He was responsible for the building of many hotels up and down the eventual path of the Florida East Coast Railway on the eastern shore of Florida, including the Ponce de León Hotel in St. Augustine (now part of Flagler College) and The Royal Poinciana Hotel in Palm Beach. But what Key West visitors over a century later may most remember him for is the building of the Casa Marina.

At the time of the opening of the Key West terminus of the Oversea Railway, Key West was often seen as an intermediate point between northern cities and ultimate destinations in Cuba, Central America, or the Caribbean. Travelers headed to Havana, for example, might expect to complete a multi-day journey by disembarking from their railroad car and re-embarking within hours on a ship poised to make the 90 mile trip south.

However, as even modern travelers will attest, connections can be the most difficult parts of a trip to manage. Therefore, relatively soon after the railroad came to Key West, a number of hotels sprung up to provide lodgings to travelers who would need to stay overnight before catching the next ship or ferry south.

Figure 5: A postcard for the Over Sea Hotel, likely intended as an intermediate stop for travelers taking the railroad to Key West and sea transportation further south. (Available under Creative Commons with attribution: Florida Keys Public Library MM00039032x.)

On a postcard from the DeWolfe and Wood Collection from the Florida Keys Public Library,[15] the Over Sea Hotel is depicted. A copy of the card in the author's collection carries a postmark of 1918 and a notation of "New Additions for 1917 Season."

The presence of women, children, and a couple in front of this well-appointed hotel suggests a degree of comfort that would make the more delicate travelers better able to rest up for the second leg of their journey, while the fact that the women are wearing light-colored garments may be a subtle form of advertising that would be appreciated by marketers even today.

Around the turn of the century, rail travel may have been the fastest and most efficient form of transportation around, but it certainly left something to be desired when it came to cleanliness. Coal-fired engines belched out great plumes of smoke which traveled back to enter passenger cabins by the open windows. It was a truism among female travelers that light-colored clothing was a foolish extravagance on a train trip, unless the wearer wanted to arrive at her destination marred by smoke. By showing women attired in light or white dresses standing in front of the Over Sea Hotel, the hotel implied that its facilities would allow guests to clean up and refresh themselves before continuing on.

Hotels like the Over Sea Hotel were strategically located to be convenient to travelers using Key West as a connecting point. The hotel's location at 919 Fleming Street put it within easy walking distance of both the terminus of the Florida East Coast Railway and of Key West Bight (now the Historic Seaport), meaning it was just a few blocks away for travelers by both land and sea. This is confirmed by the advertising copy on the reverse of the card, which indicates that the Over Sea Hotel was the "nearest hotel to railroad and steamboat station."

That the hotel was used as a stopping-off point between steamboat and rail travel is confirmed by the message written by the card's user.[16] The message reads, in part, "Estoy in Key West y la semana proxima llegaré á New York:" "I'm in Key West and next week am coming to New York."

According to the Over Sea Hotel's own advertising, it was the "Largest and Only Modern Hotel in the City," featuring all outside rooms, each with either a shared or private bath, access to hot and cold running water in every room, and access to a European plan billing system with room rates between $1 and $3 per night (a quite reasonable $17.41 to $52.24 in 2017 dollars[17]). Surely this hotel was a luxury for travelers, but it was nothing compared to what was to come.

The House by the Sea

The Casa Marina, however, was intended to be a destination unto itself. Designed by noted New York architects Thomas Hastings and John M. Carrere, the Casa Marina featured "thick, concrete wall and the spacious, high-ceilinged, wood-paneled interiors that were first conceived for the Ponce de Leon," that were characteristic of the Flagler hotels throughout Florida.[18]

In fact, the Casa Marina was intended as a tribute to Henry Flagler, who had been instrumental in giving Hastings and Carrere their start toward fame as architects. The pair, "not only specified every construction detail, but oversaw every aspect of the Casa's interior decoration, right down to the high-backed wicker armchairs in the lobby."[19]

Construction was managed by Louis Schutt, who oversaw construction logistics for the Overseas Railway and applied the same techniques to building the Casa. "After all, he reasoned, if the special concrete mix imported from Germany for the Seven Mile Bridge foundations was recommended as the best for the purpose, then the same material should also serve well as the rock solid base of one of the world's finest hotels."[20] The care is evident even today as one visits the Casa and observes the 22-inch thick walls made of steel-reinforced concrete. The concrete was "mixed with native gravel dredged from the harbor where the Overseas Railway had reached its final destination."[21] Schutt had designed the Casa to be both hurricane-resistant and luxurious.

But perhaps the most notable feature of the Casa is how well its design fits its location. Nestled into a triangular plot near the Southernmost Point, it is bordered by Reynolds Street and Seminole Street on its inland side and by 1200 feet of ocean on its beach side. The hotel was gracefully designed with a central building flanked by two angled arms that seem to embrace the beach and the walkway that leads from the front doors down to the sand. Although this walkway has changed and seen improvements over the near-century that guests have been staying at the Casa, photographic evidence proves that it has always been a palm- and greenery-flanked straight shot from the spacious lobby to the opportunity to put toes in the sand. Because of this, visitors to the Casa have always been able to have the experience of arriving at the front doors tired and travel-creased and being transported instantly to a protected enclave of sand, sun, and shore.

The Casa Marina officially opened its doors on New Year's Eve, 1920, in a party that ended past dawn in the first hours of 1921. It seemed to usher in an era of prosperity and optimism that would last nearly the entire decade, creating an entirely new climate for marketers. These new opportunities came first to the household and later to luxury travel, as technological and cultural advances gave Americans an unprecedented-to-that-point chance to have the time and money to purchase luxury products and experiences.

If a modern American reading this book were to be magically transported back in time a century to the 1920s, he or she would find a comfortable, familiar environment. Certainly, one would miss some of the modern entertainment and work tools: computers, the internet, and television would certainly top the list. However, the 1920s saw the birth of a number of modern conveniences that changed the way we live and work and, not incidentally, the amount of time we have available for leisure.

By the dawn of the 1920s, the Industrial Revolution had seen the largest amount of its impact on American society. Certainly, this is evident in the construction of the Florida East Coast Railway, which depended on an existing rail network, the manufacture of reliable steels and building products, and methods of transportation (such as the automobile) that could help transport materials and workers to job sites. But American home life had undergone a transformation as dramatic as that which took place on the factory floor.

For the first time, products were coming to market that allowed women to run a household without the constant workload that characterized previous eras and without the domestic help that was much more of an expectation for the middle and upper classes prior to this point. Inventions like the modern refrigerator and the electric toaster made food prep easier for the housewife. The refrigerator, in particular, brought a tremendous change to the way kitchens were run, eliminating the need for a messy, melting block of ice in an ice box and replacing it first with a motor-driven ice box retrofit and later with a separate appliance that featured both refrigeration and a small freezer compartment. These and similar inventions freed women (primarily) from much of the drudge work of running a household, much as the shorter shifts and greater productivity of the factory assembly line meant jobs that allowed for 40-hour weeks with greater leisure time for those who held them.

The automobile, which certainly had its role outside the home in industrial and construction operations, was well on its way to transforming American society. Although the American road system was in its infancy, featuring stretches of road that were unpaved, uneven, prone to flooding, and generally difficult to maneuver upon, the automobile gave Americans a much greater range for their travels. It also brought independence, as Americans were no longer reliant on mass transportation such as the railroad to travel long distances, although the relative comfort of railroad tracks might make this method of travel an appealing option for some years yet to come.

Changes were also coming to the national culture from movies and other mass media, hitting their heyday during this era. Motion pictures had two very important roles in driving consumption in America, specifically consumption of leisure and luxury goods and services.

The movies were the first truly synchronous experience available to the masses. Viewers in New York, Kansas City, and San Francisco could all watch silent film star Clara Bow, for example, in one of her hit movies on the same day at the same time (or, at least, within a fairly narrow timeframe of days or weeks). This meant that Americans across the country could have the same cultural experiences as peers they never met.

This synchronous dissemination of culture couldn't help but drive styles and make movie stars. Not only did many Americans learn to recognize Bow (and many others), but they clamored to use some of their new disposable income to emulate the life of these stars, choosing clothing, makeup, products, and travel destinations that they saw their film idols choose.

Advertising historian Juliann Sivulka explains the climate of the 1920s: "Perhaps more than anything else, the 1920s marked a new high point when mass-produced images in glossy magazines and Hollywood film distinctly and powerfully began to influence men's

Figure 6: Singer Rudy Vallee (R) at the Casa Marina from the Jeff Broadhead Collection at the Florida Keys Public Library. (Available under Creative Commons with attribution: Florida Keys Public Library MM00014027x.)

and especially women's self-conception, as they compared themselves to the ideals of beauty, masculinity, and femininity considered desirable at any point in time."[22]

The 1920s brought a fortuitous combination of mass communication and relative affluence to the world of marketing. Yes, the near-ubiquity of movie theaters made celebrities recognizable, but this factor alone would not be enough to boost sales of any product, service, or experience. As a counterpoint, one need only look a decade further on, during the Great Depression of the 1930s, when movies were more popular than ever, but they served primarily to allow patrons a few hours of escape from reality rather than providing a reason to purchase.

In the 1920s, however, the economic climate was quite different. The Industrial Revolution had ushered in an era of generally higher wages for the common man and the wealthy alike, while shortening work days to our more-familiar eight-hour days and 40-hour work weeks. This combination meant that consumers had more time and money for leisure activities than ever before, a situation that marketers were eager to take advantage of.

Luxury hotels like the Casa took full advantage of this. Beginning with President Warren C. Harding, who visited the Casa just three days after its opening,[23] the hotel played host to many notable artists, writes, film stars, and other notable figures throughout its first several decades.

The Casa also played into the freer, less restrictive cultural environment of the 1920s. The Casa was a home-away-from-home to a uniquely 1920s class of Americans. "They were, as novelist John Dos Passos put it, part of a 'second America,' a nation of artists, writers, actors and actresses, sports stars, musicians, journalists, dancers . . .anyone who made the break from the rigid constraints of a Victorian past and was determined to revel in the new freedoms and exuberance of the Twenties."[24] Whereas England experienced the freedom of the post-WWI generation of "Bright Young Things," America did likewise with a group of people who could afford to have fun and who saw no reason not to do so.

And what fun they had! Dancing became an unfettered way to celebrate with members of the opposite sex, with jazz music and dances like the foxtrot, the Charleston, and the Black Bottom all the rage. And, just 20 years after the death of Queen Victoria and the official end of the Victorian age, people seemed eager to shed the constraints that had bound them before the world went to war.

One of these trends was nudity, which the official Casa Marina history says the hotel "adapted [to] with equanimity by opening two rooftop sunrooms where the newly naked could bask unfettered under southern skies."[25] Once their clothes were on, guests at the Casa could partake of tennis, croquet, sport fishing, dining, and dancing.

All of this came at a surprisingly affordable price tag, especially for the newly-affluent "artists, writers, actors and actresses, sports stars, musicians, journalists, and dancers – the people who made the Twenties roar,"[26] who frequented the Casa's 175 luxurious rooms. "A double room with private bath that included three full meals per day was $9,"[27] an amount that has the same buying power as about $108 in 2016 dollars.[28]

And the meals were truly impressive. A menu from the Casa shows that dinner offered such delicacies as oysters on the half shell, lobster Newburgh, roast ribs of prime beef, fresh shrimp salad, blackberry pie, and a selection of ice cream, fruits, and nuts, among other, more pedestrian offerings.[29]

Even with all of this luxury, the economics of running a hotel and "vacation" destination were quite different in the 1920s than they are today. According to Tom Hambright, Senior Librarian for Florida History for the Monroe Public Library, the "season" for Casa Marina lasted just three months, with the hotel opening on New Year's Eve and closing at the end of March.[30] It goes a long way toward explaining to the modern eye all of the existing pictures of visitors to the Casa, sitting on its expansive porch area fully dressed in skirts and sweaters, cloche hats and fully-fashioned stockings. In fact, restricting the season to just the three coolest months on the island made a great deal of sense in this pre-air conditioning era, to take advantage of the cooler daytime temperatures and sea breezes that characterize Key West's winter.

The Casa seemed built to weather the challenges that the Great Depression era would bring. Even in the midst of economic downturn, the Casa added 25 more rooms to its offerings during the Thirties, each with the kind of solid construction that allowed the entire edifice to make it through the tragic 1935 hurricane that destroyed the Overseas Railway and was responsible for great loss of life throughout the Keys.[31]

All would not continue to be glitz and glamor for the Casa. The property would change hands repeatedly throughout the twentieth century, even closing for a time and becoming part of the lease property of the U.S. Army. It would serve as an important base through the Cuban Missile Crisis, and only later would it be revived and renovated to its former glory.

Tourism before the Great Depression

For many years, the Casa Marina and the Hotel La Concha were the only luxury hotels on the island,[32] pointing to the relatively small amount of tourism that was trickling into Key West. In fact, La Concha was immortalized in Ernest Hemingway's *To Have and Have Not*, in passages that at once show the hardscrabble life that was still evident on the island and the luxury hotel's role as an almost-literal beacon to those coming in from sea:

> Then we came to the edge of the stream and the water quit being blue and was light and greenish and inside I could see the stakes on the Eastern and Western Dry Rocks and the wireless masts at Key West and the La Concha hotel up high out of all the low houses and plenty smoke from out where they're burning garbage.[33]

However, there were at least some who saw the island's potential with a great deal of prescience. One early "snowbird" wrote an analysis in a January 1924 issue of *The Key West Citizen* detailing the potential of the transient, wintertime visitor:

> And one of these days, and it won't be long either, so many tourists will want to spend the winter here that accommodations must be provided for them, and many of them will build themselves, resulting in a boom that will send realty values sky high in Key West. It's coming; nothing can stop it, but it's coming should be hastened, and it is up to your people to do that.[34]

One hopes that the original letter-writer took his own advice and bought property on the island in 1924. His descendants are sure to have reaped the benefits.

In fact, the city was making its first forays into advertising to attract tourists. Professor Robert Kerstein notes, "the Key West Chamber of Commerce received public funds to publicize Key West via newspaper advertisements and widely distributed brochures."[35] The copy on one 1923 Chamber of Commerce publication quoted by Kerstein is worth examination:

> The view from the car windows begs description. The opalescent waters, . . . the varicolored seaweeds showing through the water, the deep-blue sky and the wonderful cloud effects, make a picture long-to-be-remembered and never-to-be forgotten by all those who are so fortunate as to make this trip.
>
> The scenery on the island is semitropical and most interesting for the tourist and visitor.
>
> The architecture of the houses, low and solidly built, gives an old-world charm and foreign atmosphere to Key West. From behind lightly closed shutters, down the long streets, one almost listens for the tinkle of a guitar or strains of La Paloma.
>
> The place has as much personality as New Orleans, an atmosphere intangible and indefinable, and its code of living, like that of all islands, is autocratic, easy unto itself.
>
> The pretty Spanish and Cuban girls as well as the lovely American maidens, and navy men in flawless white uniforms, the trim marines . . . from the barracks all form a picturesque pageant on a Key West promenade.
>
> The coffee shops, the fish markets, the 'turtle crawls' and the street vendors crying their wares, form a marvelous medley of sound and color.

Spend your winter vacation in Key West, the only FROST-FREE city in the United States."[36]

The above passage is an example of what is known as "impressionistic copy," a technique developed by copywriter Theodore MacManus.[37] Historian Juliann Sivulka notes that impressionistic copy solved a major problem with the previously-popular "reason why" copy, which sought to give customers reasons to purchase a good. Instead, impressionistic copy "extoll[s] the pleasure it would provide the purchaser." Impressionistic copy, at its finest, describes the experience of enjoying a product rather than enjoying the product itself.

MacManus's crowning achievement in impressionistic copy was the "Penalty of Leadership" ad for Cadillac,[38] which appeared just once, in the January 2, 1915, issue of *The Saturday Evening Post*. The all-text ad, broken only by a simple border and the Cadillac logo, told a story of leadership in flashes of the challenges and trials that a leader would encounter. Mocked by his peers until he succeeds, that potential for success remains his only reward. Only by implication does the reader understand that such leadership deserves a reward like a Cadillac.

Although the copy above is much more explicitly about Key West than the "Penalty of Leadership" is about Cadillac, the same impressionistic technique highlights the unique attributes of the island that can often make it feel like another world. The copy is clearly written by a copywriter with an intimate understanding of the island, but by one who also knows what features stand out to the visitor. References to the stunning views available on the drive from the mainland and the foreign-feeling architecture communicate the idea that a trip to Key West is like stepping into another world. With just a few economical words, the reader is transported into a visit that offers a laid-back lifestyle, attractive residents, and unique experiences. And, like many Key West ads of the period, the words "FROST-FREE" are highlighted with capital letters, emphasizing the attribute of the island that has always been most appealing to potential visitors during winter months.

The Power of Celebrity Endorsement

Casa Marina is an excellent demonstration of the power of celebrity endorsement as a marketing tool, even when used indirectly. Although the celebrities who spent their Key West stay at the Casa may not have lent their names to a print ad, their very presence (and appearance in newspaper photos, of course), meant that the Casa could use the power of celebrity to enhance its own reputation.

Celebrity endorsement as an advertising strategy was developed in the 1920s by noted copywriter Helen Lansdowne Resor, who has been credited with work on many of the most influential ad campaigns of the first part of the twentieth century. In 1916, she and husband Stanley Resor, president of advertising agency J. Walter Thompson (JWT), set out to develop the first research department within an advertising agency.[39]

For the first time in advertising history, market research was used to help craft copy and message in a way that would give customers a reason to buy. A fusion of quantitative research (such as measuring population, buying outlets, brand preferences, and consumer socioeconomic data) and psychology allowed the agency to craft a "creative strategy," a device used by marketers as the cornerstones of campaigns even today.[40]

Based on their work in research-driven marketing, JWT developed a number of advertising strategies that served as templates for their campaigns. One of these is the celebrity endorsement, a campaign technique that took advantage of the dissemination of mass media in the form of movies (as discussed above) and other types of media that fueled dreams of a luxurious lifestyle.

Celebrity endorsement and other forms of linking celebrity with product could arguably be called the earliest form of "lifestyle advertising." Although the term "lifestyle advertising" would not be widely used until the early 1980s, with the term reaching its peak in the mid-1990s,[41] the concept had its origin in the 1920s.

Lifestyle advertising, as the name implies, sells a certain lifestyle to the consumer that is (theoretically) available through the purchase of a product or experience, rather than just selling the product itself. Jumping ahead, the prototypical lifestyle brand of the 1980s, Ralph Lauren Polo, makes the distinction clear. Some 60 or more years after the construction of Casa Marina, Ralph Lauren's Polo brand would sell the "preppy" lifestyle to its consumers, with all its implications of affluence, good breeding, fine education, and polished manners. This would, of course, be more lucrative than selling an undifferentiated collection of polo shirts and khaki trousers.

In the 1920s, however, celebrities could accomplish the same thing for a brand, and consumers were poised to act. The vision of a movie star or well-loved politician lounging in the breezy lobby or on the veranda of the Casa would communicate to the everyday consumer that a lifestyle of affluence, luxury, and refinement was theirs for the taking, if only for a few days while on vacation. And, with extra discretionary income in their pockets and an expanding slate of transportation options, the number of people who could temporarily live the good life in Key West was on the rise.

The Luxury of Pan Am

The Casa Marina was not the only travel luxury to be found in Key West during the 1920s. In 1927, Pam American Airways (Pan Am) was founded in Key West, and the island became home to the country's first international airport, thanks to Pan Am's regular flights to and from Havana, Cuba.

It wasn't all about Key West, however. The original Key West Pan Am connection came in 1927, when the airline sought to secure "the coveted U.S. Post Office contract for the Foreign Airmail Contract to carry the U.S. Mail from Key West, Florida, to Havana, Cuba – and the great potential for expansion of air routes beyond to Latin America."[42] With much wheeling and dealing – and not a small amount of management of logistics – Pan Am was able to satisfy the terms of the deal to demonstrate the ability to deliver mail on the last possible day, October 19, 1927. Just nine days later, Pan Am flight number one departed Key West for Havana, making the first scheduled American international air service flight.[43]

Pam Am was one of Key West's truly national and nominally international victories in the battle to capture the growing travel market. "Pam Am, which opened its first corporate offices in Key West, was being expanded each year by is founder, Juan Trippe. Pam Am planes left Miami daily for the Key West flight, in those days [a] one hour and twenty minute trip."[44] The flight was described as "comfortable and interesting."[45]

Soon, Pan Am made a strategic decision to move its U.S. airmail terminus to Miami, doubling the mileage to fly to Havana and consequently doubling the payout from the per-mile rate specified in the contract. A general move of the international travel traffic from Key West to Miami had begun almost before Key West had become established as the hub for air travel to points south.

Subsequent travel-related advertising would highlight the Miami terminus for Pan Am's commercial flight, but this advertising would also emphasize all of the destinations throughout the Caribbean, Mexico, and northern South America.

The Key West airport would never become the sprawling hub that Miami would be, as evidenced by the modern facilities that, even after an upgrade, still boast passenger disembarking on the tarmac and a "First Call" bar that travelers can patronize as they wait for their luggage. However, these same travelers can still visit the first Pan Am office, where the first Pan Am airline ticket was purchased, on Whitehead Street, where the building has become a successful restaurant and microbrewery.

By the end of the 1920s, Key West was enjoying its literal place in the sun with visits from A-list celebrities, bohemian artists, and vacationers of all stripes. But everything would change with the arrival of the Great Depression.

Jennifer Patterson Lorenzetti

CHAPTER 3: OBSERVING THE HEMINGWAYS
Ernest Hemingway and the Great Depression

By the dawning of the Great Depression, Key West had started to experience the tension between tourism and local culture that would persist through the remainder of the 20th century. And this tension was felt and explained by no less august a resident that Ernest Hemingway, whose distrust of the government and desire for privacy met up in objections to the tourist trade that are remembered today.

FERA and the Great Depression

The Great Depression came as a shock to Key West, much as it likely did to many communities that had spent the 1920s in affluence only to see much of the population plunge into poverty with the economic collapse. The Federal Emergency Relief Administration (FERA) jumped in to help the small island, and it did so not just with money but with a public relations campaign designed to replace the traditional industries of sponging, salvaging, and fishing/turtling with tourism.

Marketing collateral aimed at attracting tourists were not shy about explaining the island's transition to a tourist economy. In a selection of brochure pages preserved in the Otto Hirzel scrapbook[46] about Key West, maintained by the Florida Keys Public Library, copy trumpets the traditional reasons for visiting the island: the perpetual summer-like climate, the semi-tropical nature and beauty of the island, and the benefits to those healing from "sinus trouble, arthritis, rheumatism, [and] cardiac disorders." It also explicitly invited "the tired business man, the sportsman, the lover of the outdoors, the artist, the writer – in short, any one [sic] seeking a change from the normal routine." On another page, however, the brochure gave a fairly unvarnished picture of what the Depression meant to the island.

Guidebooks from the period of FERA administration also were not shy about trumpeting the perceived triumph of the agency in rescuing the island from its economy. In *Key West Guide Book: An Aid to the Visitor – Fall and Winter 1935-1936*, published by the Key West Administration, the story of the economic collapse and the arrival of the government is told in unflinching terms:[47]

> One hundred years ago, Key West was the richest city in Florida and one of the wealthiest per capita in the United States. In June, 1934, it was one of the poorest. The history of that of that century, 1834-1934, will furnish more than one moral to the investigator with an eye for symbols, and, in the ruin of industry on an island of four miles square he will find the same forces at work that destroyed the prosperity of a nation.

The guide goes on to describe a situation in 1934 that makes the reader wonder quite why anyone would care to visit the island in 1935, when this volume was published.

> In 1934 the city was in a desperate condition. All its industries were dead; its government was completely bankrupt; its municipal employees were facing starvation; it had defaulted on its bonds and could no longer function; rents and taxes were no longer paid; and a large proportion of the population was on relief. With refuse mounting there was danger of an epidemic; anaemia, caused by malnutrition, was spreading among the people; the poor, who had always been poor enough, now went in rags.

All of this is a lead-in to trumpet the triumphs of Julius Stone, the FERA Administrator for Florida, who is largely credited with rescuing the island's finances by changing its primary industry from the original salvage, harvest, and production industries to tourism. The guide details a simultaneous program of promoting the island while it was "given a thorough cleaning" that rendered the island "hygienically safe." The Public Works of Art Project (PWAP) provided artists to help boost the aesthetics of the island and the artistic opportunities available in the form of galleries and art classes.

The guide wastes no time in declaring the rehabilitation and turn to tourism a success. "During the winter, wholly as a result of the tourist business, the number of persons on relief rolls dropped approximately twenty-five per cent – and this was the first season of the experiment," it crows. It also notes that between 35,000 and 40,000 tourists visited the island that first season, with about 3,000 staying for the winter. FERA and Julius Stone were clearly eager to claim victory.

Stone was nothing if not committed to tourism, and he arguably made one of the biggest impacts of the twentieth century on how Key West was perceived by the U.S., second only to Henry Flagler. Professor Robert Kerstein recounts the story that Stone argued against developing any new industry in Key West other than tourism, even blocking a proposal by the mayor of Key West to "petition Congress for authorization [of Key West] as a foreign trade zone." "It would be a mistake to attempt to make [Key West] anything except a resort city. If you brought in one or two industries, they would drive away the tourists. The industries would not support it, and then it would be neither fish nor fowl," Stone said.[48]

FERA took advantage of the Depression to make an argument to northerners to entice them to visit the island. Clearly, this was a difficult sales proposition, because not everyone was noticeably better off than the island of Key West, and travel south on vacation was a luxury many could not afford. And, more important, the Conchs were not always enthusiastic about the influx of so many tourists into

their home.
Invasions of Privacy

Noted American writer Ernest Hemingway was not the first or the last to call Cayo Hueso home, nor was he the famous writer who lived the longest on the island; that honor goes to Tennessee Williams, who began visiting the island in 1941 and lived there until his death in 1983.

But it is Hemingway's unique personality, combined with his journalistic style of writing, that causes many to immediately associate the island with his story. Given his ability to make fiction read like fact, Hemingway is considered to bring a degree of truthfulness to his writing that he may or may not have been intended at any given time. Nonetheless, one can look at his Key West experience as portrayed through his writing to understand the tensions at play on the island.

Hemingway came to the island in 1928 and moved permanently there in 1931, right at the start of the Great Depression. In one of the more notable examples of taking advantage of fluctuations in the Key West real estate market, he found salvage magnate Asa Tift's beautiful two-story house at 907 Whitehead Street[49] standing empty, and he purchased it for $8,000 in back taxes from the City of Key West. He lived there with second wife Pauline and sons Gregory ("Gigi") and Patrick from the time of the purchase of the house until 1940. At that time, he moved to Cuba with his third wife, Martha Gelhorn.

The house soon became the site of many legendary happenings that add color to the story of the author's life. A white ceramic trough sits in the back yard as a catch-basin for a fountain built from a large urn; this basin is reputedly one of the urinals from the original Sloppy Joe's (now the site of Captain Tony's Saloon) that Hemingway and friends removed and relocated when Sloppy Joe Russell was forced to move his tavern from Greene Street to Duval Street.

Additionally, the backyard sports a pool that is decorated with a penny embedded in the concrete. Lore holds that Hemingway

Figure 7: 907 Whitehead Street, originally owned by Asa Tift and later by Ernest Hemingway. From the Scott DeWolfe Collection at the Florida Keys Public Library. (Available under Creative Commons with attribution: Florida Keys Public Library MM00042282x.)

returned home from a trip to find Pauline having a pool put in and threw the penny into the still-wet concrete, inviting her to spend his last cent while she was redecorating. (The penny, visitors will note, is rather well-placed and embedded to be the result of a random toss.) And, in a burst of home décor fashion that even modern visitors will rue, Pauline removed the ceiling fans from the sub-tropical house, electing to install chandeliers that were much more fashionable, if much less practical.

Regardless of Hemingway's larger-than-life reputation on the island, he clearly desired his privacy. In the depths of the Great Depression, FERA officials printed a tourist map of the island that clearly marked "Hemingway's House," a move the author abhorred. Shortly thereafter, he hired a masonry wall built around the property; the wall still stands.

Even more critical is his perception that attempts to turn Key West into a tourist destination would drive out the locals and bleed the unique culture from the island, a concern that you can still hear from those who call Key West home. Hemingway put his concerns into his characters' mouths, most notably with this passage from *To Have and Have Not*,[50] which features Key West and was written while he lived on the island.

> ...my family's going to eat as long as anybody eats. What they're trying to do is starve you Conchs out of here so they can burn down the shacks and put up apartments and make this a tourist town. That's what I hear. I hear they're buying up lots, and then after the poor people are starved out and gone somewhere else to starve some more they're going to come in and make it into a beauty spot for tourists.

Hemingway was not the only artist upset about the new emphasis on tourism. In a letter to a friend, Katy Dos Passos, wife of writer John Dos Passos, was unapologetic in her frustrations with the FERA occupation of the island and the resulting focus on making it a tourist haven: "The New Dealers are here . . . and Key West is now a Greenwich Village Nightmare. . .they're painting murals on the café walls, and weaving baskets, and cutting down plants and trees, and renting all the homes (with Washington money) and arranging sight-seeing tours, and building apartments for tourists so they can observe the poor Hemingways . . . There is even a band of fake Cubans with velvet pants and red sashes that meets the train every day."[51]

The concerns cited by Hemingway and others were not without merit; indeed, one look at the island today makes plain the emphasis on shiny new rental properties for tourists, arguably built at the expense of housing for the Conchs, who are increasingly forced to look one, two, or more islands north to find affordable housing. Hemingway's own house, likely much to his chagrin were he alive, now sports a line of tourists queuing up through the gate of the masonry fence, awaiting their chance to gawk at his bedroom, his

Figure 8: Postcard showing arrival and unloading of a turtle boat, likely either at the future site of the Key West Aquarium or at the Turtle Kraals, from the Florida Keys Public Library. (Available under Creative Commons with attribution: Florida Keys Public Library MM00012833.)

writing room, and his makeshift fountain. But, like it or not, the shift to an emphasis on tourism had begun with the efforts of Julius Stone, and they continue today.

The Reinvention of the Island

The Great Depression was the official start of Key West's shift from harvest-oriented industries to a focus on tourism, and the first to feel this change was the Key West Aquarium, still open for tours. The site, located at the foot of Duval Street on what is now Mallory Square, was ideally situated for its original role in the sponging and turtle harvesting industries. Boats could pull up from their day's work and unload their harvest onto the weathered wooden docks, ready for processing in nearby buildings. Illustrations from the era shows the docks loaded down with piles of sponge and bodies of turtles, ready for the next stage in their journey north.

The Key West Aquarium was built on this site, making it the first tourist attraction in Key West and likely the first such aquarium facility in the country. The building features a ruffled front façade

Figure 9: Construction of Key West Aquarium circa 1935. (Available under Creative Commons with attribution: Florida Keys Public Library MM00088834x.)

very typical of the late Art Deco era of architecture, and was designed around open-air holding tanks that are still in use today.[52] A "curio shop," the precursor of the many tourist-oriented souvenir shops that dot Key West today, completed the installation.[53]

The aquarium was designed to take advantage of the natural assets of Key West, namely the variety of sea life living in the immediate environs. Copy accompanying the photo[54] in Figure 9 explains the attractions that were anticipated at the time:

> Key West Open Air Aquarium under construction. Nearly a thousand varieties of tropical fish will be seen in the Key West Tropical Open Air Aquarium, now being completed by the Florida Emergency Relief Administration as one move to accentuate the many attractions of the little island city at the extreme southern end of the Florida Keys. Tropical fish abound in the waters of the Gulf and Atlantic, surrounding Key West, and here at the water's edge they will be kept near

Figure 10: Key West Aquarium circa 1950. (Available under Creative Commons with attribution: Florida Keys Public Library MM00039510x.)

their natural habitats. Open, circulating salt water will be pumped from the sea into the fish tanks providing an abundant supply of natural water for the beautiful fish of the tropical salt waters. It will be the only tropical open air aquarium in the world where no artificial temperatures or atmosphere will have to be maintained.

Like many Depression-era projects, the Aquarium was designed to provide jobs for the recently-unemployed, of which there were many in Key West. The Aquarium would help with that problem both by providing jobs and by attracting tourists to the island.

The Aquarium was designed by Dr. Robert O. Van Deusen, Superintendent of the Fairmount Aquarium in Philadelphia.[55] The Civil Works Administration (CWA) and the Federal Emergency Relief Administration (FERA), both part of President Franklin Delano Roosevelt's "alphabet soup" of Depression-relief programs, paid for the design and construction of the Aquarium. The Public Works Project Administration commissioned a group of seven artists to paint murals that would appear around the island, each for a salary of $35 per week. According to the Aquarium's official in-house historical signage:

> Italian-born artist Alfred Crimi arrived in August of 1934 eager to begin his assigned project of creating murals for the new Aquarium. Crimi was highly-skilled in the art of vero fresco (painting on wet plaster), the medium he would use for the Aquarium murals. He made several trips to the Dry Tortugas to observe and study local fishermen laying their nets and pulling in the catch. Crimi spent eight months in Key West, one of the most memorable experiences of his career.[56]

The murals are stunning examples of what is often referred to as "WPA style" art. WPA style art references Art Deco with its broad swaths of color and simplification of detail. The simplification inherent in the Art Deco style made it ideal for public works projects across the country, because these programs were more about putting men to work than they were about creating detailed, photo-realistic art. The style was kind to a range of artistic skills, but it really shines under the brush of a talented artist.

Much WPA art focused on the efforts of the working man, showing the triumph of labor and industry, an important balm for the souls of the many unemployed. The Crimi murals celebrate the maritime industries of Key West, with some showing heavily muscled men working in the fishing industry.

Although the Crimi murals were destroyed during World War II due to neglect, they have been recreated for the Aquarium, and the reproductions hang on the walls to this day. Their depictions of muscled arms, tanned faces, and nets full of the day's catch could easily be used to illustrate Hemingway's *To Have and Have Not*, so beautifully do they evoke the feeling of the island of this period. In effect, WPA style murals like those created by Crimi serve an important advertising function. The simplicity of the Art Deco-inspired style encourages the focus on a single message and conveys it with maximum visual impact. In the case of the Crimi murals,

Figure 11: Reproduction of an Alfred D. Crimi mural for the Key West Aquarium, 1998. (Available under Creative Commons with attribution: Florida Keys Public Library MM00033840x.)

visitors to the Key West Aquarium could see a tribute to the hard working inhabitants of the island and understand the industries that were typical for the area. The murals functioned as a form of advertising that emphasized the traditional culture of the island and doubtless made visitors feel more of the flavor of this exotic destination.

The WPA was not exclusively about employing artists, however. The program also offered a Writers' Program, which, in part, published guide books to introduce the public to the culture and attractions of Key West. In *A Guide to Key West*, originally published in 1941 and in its second edition by 1949, the WPA writers described the island in an honest way:[57]

> At first glance, this may seem a dilapidated city; small native dwellings and balconied houses are for the most part gray and unpainted. These venerable structures, however, their framework put together with trenails or wooden pegs, and anchored deep in coral rock, have withstood the few hurricanes and high winds that have struct this island city. The absence of chimneys is noticeable: the mild winters make heating systems unnecessary.

The guide goes on to trace the island's tourist trade back to the Great Depression, again with proper credit given to the architect of this change in focus. The section then continues describing the island in ways that make the uninitiated visitor feel as if he or she is visiting a foreign land:[58]

> As Key West became tourist-conscious in the 1930s under the stimulus of Federal relief and lending agencies, streets were repaired, yards and vacant lots were cleared, and many old houses took new coats of paint. This effective beautification program was initiated under the direction of Julius Stone, then state head of the Florida ERA
> Streets in the business section are practically deserted during early afternoons. Shops and residences are shuttered, and the siesta of the tropics is in order. The few pedestrians are seldom in a hurry; there are no streetcars or city busses; automobiles and bicycles are the popular means of conveyance.

The same guide goes on to introduce the reader to the multiethnic population of the island, explaining that "the majority of residents are descendants of pioneers from Virginia, New England, and the West Indies," but that the island is also made up of "'Conchs,' Latins, and Negroes," many of whom made their way to Key West via migration that each group made to the Bahamas.[59] Interestingly, the guide prepares the reader for the various accents he or she will encounter on a visit, a task that is likely unnecessary for today's more sophisticated traveler. "Both white and Negro immigrants from the Bahamas speak with a cockney accent and retain cockney words and phrases,"[60] the author writes. The guide also gives some attention to the dialects of the fishermen and ship's carpenters that frequent the waterfront bight area, particularly noting a specific accent: "The long 'o's,' dropping and adding 'h's,' substituting 'w' for 'v,' all these habits of speech make for a picturesque and charming patois."[61]

Publications that originated a bit closer to home, however, exhibit the love that the native Conchs have always had for their island. In a 1939 guide called *Go to Sea Key West*, the copy waxes poetic in describing the wonders of the island:[62]

> We drink the best water in the world; it comes directly from heaven – and there is plenty of it . . . We swim in the Gulf of Mexico and five minutes later can take a dip in the Atlantic Ocean . . . . We eat at side-walk cafes and dance beneath a tropic moon . . . We laugh, we sing, we are a happy lot of healthy people. . . We have in our midst many famous writers and artists and political celebrities who spend at least part of the year here.

If the description of the lifestyle of the natives and regulars were not sufficient to attract the new visitor, the writers continue to describe the island in words that are understandably and excusably florid:[63]

> You will want to linger long in Key West, held by the magnetism of this luminous island, where truly tropical

conditions prevail . . . You will be captivated by its romantic background, where tales of pirates and buried treasure are laid on foundations of truth.

Overall, the marketing and public relations materials inviting visitors to Key West underwent a shift during the Great Depression. Instead of prior decades' efforts to make the business case for a visit to Key West, citing its strategic importance, Depression-era marketing relied more and more on the intrinsic benefits of the subtropical climate and the unique attributes of the island's culture.

Writing in the *Miami Herald*, a 1936 reporter described the situation this way: "Visitors in Key West say that they could go into many other tourist cities blindfolded, and having had their blindfolds removed, would be unable to tell what city it was; while if they went through the same test in Key West, they would recognize immediately the island city – by its houses, its strange little naturally floral decorated lanes, or by some other 'something' which makes the city Key West."[64] The sentiment is still true today; Conchs and transplants alike worry about maintaining the historic housing and the traditional feel of the island culture, and the entrance of another chain store or hotel is often met with derision and a desire to fight to maintain the unique culture of the island.

The Labor Day Hurricane

If it weren't enough that the Keys were buffeted by the Great Depression, in 1935 they were hit by a meteorological event with far-reaching effect. On Labor Day weekend, 1935, a category 5 hurricane hit the Keys, centered on Matecumbe Key. The United States would not see a hurricane of this strength hit the coast again until August, 1969, when Hurricane Camille hit Mississippi.

The damage was tremendous, but the loss of life was staggering. Over 400 people lost their lives in this hurricane, including over 250 World War I veterans. According to author Stuart B. McIver, "Whole families of old-time Conchs were wiped out. Even more shocking to the nation was the death of some two hundred veterans of World War I. The men had been given temporary relief jobs working on the

Overseas Highway that would one day connect Key West with the mainland."⁶⁵

Once again, Ernest Hemingway took pen in hand to lend color to the nation's understanding of the event, particularly the effect that the hurricane had on the veterans who were down on their luck due to the Depression and working tough manual labor jobs in the sweltering heat. Writing in *The New Masses*, in a piece titled "Who Murdered the Vets?" Hemingway gave a scathing indictment of the federal government which, he believed, left those who had already served their country in war in a situation that carried just as much risk of loss of life.

> It is not necessary to go into the deaths of the civilians and their families since they were on the Keys of their own free will; they made their living there, had property and knew the hazards involved. But the veterans had been sent there; they had no opportunity to leave, nor any protection against hurricanes; and they never had a chance for their lives.⁶⁶

Hemingway blamed the government for placing veterans in a hurricane zone where a severe storm such as this one could bring risks equivalent to those faced in combat. And he was also obviously deeply affected by the personal nature of the tragedy; a veteran of World War I (as a Red Cross ambulance driver) and resident of Key West himself, he had grown to know many of the veterans who lost their lives personally, and the aftermath was obviously deeply scarring for him:

> I'd known a lot of them at Josie Grunt's place [Sloppy Joe's] and around the town when they would come in for pay day, and some of them were punch drunk and some of them were smart; some had been on the bum since the Argonne almost and some had lost their jobs the year before last Christmas; some had wives and some couldn't remember; some were good guys and others put their pay checks in the Postal Savings and then came over to cadge in on the drinks when

better men were drunk; some liked to fight and others liked to walk around the town; and they were all what you get after a war. . . . But I would like to make whoever sent them there carry just one out through the mangroves or turn one over that lay in the sun along the fill, or tie five together so they won't float out, or smell that smell you thought you'd never smell again with luck. But now you know there isn't any luck when rich bastards make a war. The lack of luck goes on until all who take part in it are gone.[67]

Clearly, the loss of life in the 1935 Labor Day hurricane was devastating; focus on property damage would come later, once the bodies were retrieved and buried. But once the focus shifted to property, it was clear that the disaster meant the end of an era. The railroad bed for the Key West Extension of the Florida East Coast Railway had been irreparably damaged, and no plans were made for repair. While work had already begun on an Overseas Highway route to Key West that was tailored for the needs of automobiles, the destruction of the railroad lines meant that the original land means of travel to Key West was forever gone. From now on, travelers to Key West would make their journey primarily by automobile or by air, a condition that would last for the remainder of the twentieth century and beyond.

However, there was a change in public presentation of the island in progress. Under the management of FERA, the island was no longer marketing itself as a jumping-off point for businessmen wanting to partake of trade in the Caribbean and Central America. Instead, visitors learned about a local culture that was no less hard-working but which was firmly anchored in the island environment. From this point forward, visitors would be invited to Key West to experience what the island had to offer rather than being enticed to use it as the keystone of a business venture. Island culture had officially become a commodity to attract tourists rather than investors, bringing transient money rather than permanent investment. And nothing opened up the island – to say nothing of

Figure 12: Screencap of Chevrolet newsreel showing the road bed of what would become U.S. 1 with a 1935 Chevy handling the bounce-inducing terrain. From CHEVROLET LEADER NEWS, Vol. 1, No. 2, 1935. (Author's collection.)

the United States – like the robust car culture that would develop in the 20th century.

"See the U.S.A.…."

Although the Chevrolet division of General Motors would not file for copyright on its famous jingle "See the U.S.A. in Your Chevrolet" until 1950, the spirit of the cars being used to traverse the nation and travel to all of its corners was already alive and well in 1935 during the Great Depression. As part of a series of newsreels[68] released by the company under the name *Chevrolet Leader News*, one such installment featured a new 1935 Chevrolet bouncing its way down the unfinished road bed of U.S. 1, which would become the main arterial into Key West following the original path of the Florida East Coast Railroad. The highway would officially open in 1938.

The newsreel functions as both an advertisement for buying a Chevy and for visiting the island of Key West. As the voice-over explains the logistical challenges of visiting the island – with the once-impressive railroad service now seen as a limitation with its once a day service – the Chevy is shown driving over the road beds and even cruising along the railroad tracks without disturbing the car's occupants.

Once the car arrives in Key West, the voice-over emphasizes that the roads are completely finished on the island, and that a Chevy will allow visitors to navigate in style and comfort. The voice-over script also emphasizes that the island "soon will be swarming with tourists and fishermen," giving a sense of urgency to the call to visit. The implication is clear: a 1935 Chevy, decidedly a luxury purchase during the height of the Depression, will allow the owner to access parts of the country unseen by many but will also allow them to fit seamlessly into island life once they have arrived in Key West. It also marks an important transition from the days when journeying to Key West took time – by rail or by boat – to the days when most visitors would come by car or plane and leave just as expeditiously.

Road's End

As the 1930s marched onward, examples of advertising collateral showed a continuity of messaging with prior years with an evolving style.

In a brochure from Otto Hirzel's scrapbook maintained by the Florida Keys Public Library, we see an aerial image of the island similar to those seen during Flagler's time.[69] The island is depicted from its southernmost corner, showing the railroad and the chain of keys disappearing north into the ocean. Only the current "Old Town" and "Midtown" sections of the island are pictured, as the salt flats are still under water. The inclusion of this brochure next to a WPA map of the island in Hirzel's scrapbook indicates that it likely was produced in the 1930s.

However, where previous advertising showed Key West as the gateway to business opportunities further south, the messaging now shows the island as a destination unto itself. "All Roads End at Key West Florida" proclaims the brochure headline, with the subhead still emphasizing the subtropical climate by calling it "The Paradise of America." Echoing the extreme verticality of the Art Deco style of the 1920s, a single palm tree climbs the right hand side of the brochure, drawing the reader's eye north to south and back again on the island map while also emphasizing both headline and subhead.

Although many programs, including the WPA, were initiated as part of FDR's "alphabet soup" of initiatives to lift the country out of depression, the fact remains that nothing spurs the economy like a war. The beginning of World War II sparked the need for massive increases in employment and industry across the country. It also allowed Key West to focus its efforts on one of its original industries, being a home to the U.S. Navy.

Figure 13: All Roads End at Key West Florida, according to this 1930s brochure. (Available under Creative Commons with attribution: Florida Keys Public Library MM41339-13x.)

CHAPTER 4: INTERMEZZO
Key West and the Armed Services

Before Key West was a city, before Florida was a state, the island was an important base for the navy. Strategically, Key West sits in an ideal position from which to police parts of the Atlantic Ocean, the Gulf of Mexico, and the Caribbean.

Key West was not always the tropical paradise that some believe it to be today, and early settlers had to have a certain amount of grit to look at the island and see a life, let alone a livelihood. "Cayo Hueso (Key West) was an inhospitable coral isle, perched on the edge of a very dangerous reef. It was an island of wading birds, mangroves, mosquito clouds, and a thriving population of turtles," says an exhibit by the Key West Art and Historical Society, which further explains that early settlers had to deal with "hurricanes, fires, disease, and pirate raids."[70] However, "naval officers described Key West as an ideal harbor and recognized its military value."[71] It was this military value that encouraged the development of one of Key West's first "industries" as a strategic point for the navy in the Caribbean.

In an illustration from the April 18, 1874, issue of *Harper's Weekly*,[lxxii] two men are depicted standing atop West Martello, watching a very optimistic portrayal of the fleet in the harbor. Notable to this illustration is the presence of swampland and brush grown up nearly to the base of the tower, which stands connected by

Figure 14: Two men stand atop West Martello observing the fleet in the harbor with Fort Taylor in the distance. (Available under Creative Commons with attribution: Florida Keys Public Library MM00041084x.)

a dirt track to Fort Zachary Taylor.

In fact, the military, particularly the Navy, has always been something of a stabilizing presence Key West, a transient population that nonetheless stays for an extended period of time and becomes part of the community, located somewhere between native-born Conch and mere vacationer. Much like college towns rely upon the regular come and go of their student populations, Key West has always relied upon and catered to its residents from the Navy.

The strategic value of Forts Zachary Taylor, East Martello, and West Martello diminished after the end of the Civil War, and the value of a base in Key West for those involved in shipping also diminished once larger, faster ships with a greater fuel capacity made it unnecessary to stop in Key West or New Orleans for refueling before continuing on into the Caribbean or through the Panama Canal. Nonetheless, the Navy continued to maintain a substantial presence on the island.

The Navy brought a number of changes to some old landmarks on the island. The Custom House, built in 1891, received a very practical sort of facelift in 1918 at the request of the Navy, with the beautiful veranda and the archways of porch closed off to use those spaces for postal operations.[73] The biggest changes, however, took place at when the Navy took control of that building in the 1920s.

According to research by the Key West Art and Historical Society, "at the close of the First World War, the Commandant of the Seventh Naval District was urging construction of a new government building in Key West so the U.S. Navy could take possession of the Custom House for offices and their Civil Service Department."[74] Changes to the interior made the building much more suitable as office space, setting up for a renovation that would take place in the late 20th Century that would restore the elegance and grandeur of the building. However, for the time being, what the Navy wanted, the Navy got.

World War II

In what might be seen as a continual tug of war between Key West as a military base and Key West as a tourist haven, the military uses of the island almost always win out. Certainly, this was true during World War II, which would bring a renewed focus on the military to Key West. However, the island first would see a last whirl of luxury before the seriousness of war descended.

Histories of both world wars are filled with tales of citizens who optimistically predict a quick victory and near-immediate end to the conflict, allowing people to opt to continue their pre-war behaviors. This kind of denial or cognitive dissonance is quite common, and it was on display in Key West as the country prepared to enter the second world war.. Even as war raged in Europe, the famous and the wealthy gathered at Casa Marina to usher in the new year 1941. The official Casa Marina history quotes the *Key West Citizen* in saying that "everybody that mattered in Key West was there," describing how "the beautifully gowned and faultlessly groomed ladies danced with their escorts on the gaily illumined Casa Marina patio."[75] Clearly, there was still some glamour and luxury to be enjoyed before December 7, when the attack on Pearl Harbor would introduce a new era of austerity.

But even the elegant Casa could not remain insulated from the realities of war once the United States entered the fray. The U.S. Navy bought the Casa and turned it into officer's quarters, and the entire island, just like the entire nation, turned it's thoughts to war. But those affected could not help but notice the change. As the official Casa Marina history explains:

> For the first time since Henry Flagler's dream, the progression of events he had hoped for and planned had come to an end. His railway was wreckage, his hotel had closed its doors to the public. And although it took a second world war to do it, Casa Marina's closing, more than any other single event, told Key Westers their community might never be quite the same again.[76]

After all of the efforts during the Great Depression to turn Key West into America's Caribbean get-away, the island put on the brakes in 1943 to better accommodate wartime needs. "[T]he military presence became so strong that by the winter of 1943 the Key West Chamber of Commerce urged tourists to stay away, the military having filled all of the available accommodations,"[77] writes Professor Robert Kerstein. Of course, Americans were not exactly expecting to be on the move that year anyway. 1943 marked one of the low points for production of consumer luxuries during the war, and the government even disallowed the production of automobiles for non-military, commercial sale.

Kerstein points out other ways that life in Key West changed around military needs during WWII:

> For example, the addition of minefields meant that no private boats, other than those of commercial fishermen, were allowed in the water around the town. The *Citizen* periodically notified the townspeople to leave their window open an inch or two so that the gunshots sounded during military drills would not shatter them. And Key West was perhaps the only town in the United States where immigration officers checked everyone who boarded a bus to leave town.[78]

Harry Truman and the Little White House

The military has always been a presence in Key West, but, for two terms in office, the Commander in Chief made Key West his secondary base of operations often enough that part of the Key West Naval Station became known as "Truman's Little White House." The web site of the Little White House tells the tale of a president who served through the end of World War II, the U.S. atomic bomb attacks on Hiroshima and Nagasaki, and the post-war economic boom and recovery:

From August 16 to September 2, 1946, President Truman tried to rest by sailing to Hamilton, Bermuda. Unfortunately for the President, rough seas left him seasick and not too rested. By late fall, the President had developed a lingering cold that seemed to be getting worse. Fleet Admiral Chester Nimitz, having just inspected the Key West Naval Station, suggested Quarters A in Key West as a secure, warm retreat. The President came for a week of relaxation and promised to return. Return he did, for a total of eleven presidential working vacations and five post- presidential trips. Truman claimed Key West was his second favorite place on earth, only surpassed by his hometown of Independence, Missouri.[79]

The visits during Truman's terms in office were relatively extensive, most lasting for a week or more, and two lasting about a month each. The post-presidential visits allowed Truman the opportunity to take his family to various locations up and down the Keys, with each visit including a stop in Key West. On one such visit, in March of 1968, the Truman family stayed at the Casa Marina, becoming one more celebrity family to grace the beautiful 1920s property.

Truman was not the only president to visit Key West and the Little White House. Presidents Eisenhower, Kennedy, Carter, and Clinton have all visited, and, "in 2001, Secretary of State Colin Powell led international peace talks between the presidents of Azerbaijan and Aremenia" at the house.[80]

In between official visits, the Little White House is open to the public, being yet another example of a Key West facility that is both an integral, functioning part of the island and a tourist attraction. Visitors of a certain age will delight in the décor from the Truman era, featuring rattan furniture and textiles reminiscent of the era.

The Cuban Missile Crisis

Key West's economy has always expanded and contracted to accommodate the needs of the military, and at no time was this more evident than at the dawn of the 1960s. By 1960, "approximately 57 percent of the male labor force in Key West was in the military,"[81] writes Kerstein. The military forces in Key West increased temporarily during the Cuban Missile Crisis in 1962, with the southernmost point in the U.S. necessarily becoming heavily involved in the activities involving neighboring Cuba.

Many of the resources of Key West were dedicated to fighting the short-lived but high-tension conflict. Prior to the crisis, the Army had leased the Casa Marina from its owners, and the former luxury hotel remained an important base, as did the Naval Air Station on Boca Chica, housing code-breaking activities. Other resources were pressed into service as well, but perhaps the most visually arresting was the unfurling of concertina wire onto the beaches, to be used as machine gun nests manned by Marines.[82] The effect was evocative of scenes from the Normandy invasion during World War II, certainly not the image Key West wanted impressed on the minds of northerners for years to come.

While the island may have been concerned in the short term about the fight against communism coming to the Western Hemisphere, a more long term concern was the impact that the crisis would have on tourism. Kerstein explains:

> When President John F. Kennedy visited Key West that November, Mayor C.B. Harvey presented him with a gold key to the city that differed from the keys usually presented to visiting dignitaries. Harvey noted that the key symbolized the 'strain which

Figure 15: Concertina wire on Smathers Beach during the Cuban Missile Crisis, 1962. (Available under Creative Commons with attribution: Florida Keys Public Library MM00046461x.)

the Cuban crisis has put on the Key West economy' due to the drop in tourism. In late October, the Chamber of Commerce arranged for 'Miss Florida' to visit the community, where she was treated to a fishing trip and visits to Key West's nightspots in hopes of showing potential tourists that Key West was available for their vacations.[83]

Kerstein continues by noting that the island's tourism community also took an even longer-term view of the situation, realizing that the resulting embargo of Cuba which cut off decades of easy back-and-forth between the two islands could mean an increase in tourism concentrated in Key West alone.[84] In fact, this would turn out to be the case. On February 8, 1963, President John F. Kennedy prohibited travel from the U.S. to Cuba and made financial and commercial transactions with Cuba illegal, an expansion of the economic embargo that begin in 1960. This, the longest-running trade embargo in U.S. history, effectively cut off travel from the U.S. to Cuba until 2009, when President Barack Obama began to ease travel restrictions. However, the half century between the two events was long enough to solidify Key West's position at the end of the road for U.S. travelers.

For the first time since Flager's railroad pulled into Key West half a century before, Key West would no longer look south and position itself as a jumping off point to the Caribbean, with Cuba being the easiest first step south. For another half a century to come, Key West would be the terminus for most tourists headed south from the mainland, especially those who wanted the tropical flavor without the bother of passports and political strife.

CHAPTER 5: FAMILY FUN
The 1950s and the Birth of the Family Vacation

The end of World War II brought important changes to the U.S. economy. After all, the country had just endured a decade-long depression during which consumer spending was at a low, thanks to high unemployment and a lack of disposable income. Families moved into multi-generational housing, couples delayed marriage, young people either forewent higher education or gambled that a vocational degree could help them to find work, and everything from clothing to radios to automobiles was repaired and re-repaired to make the goods last as long as possible.

Following the depression, WWII brought a different kind of economic crisis. Suddenly, the country was not just fully employed but arguably over-employed. Not only did nearly all men have jobs, thanks to military service for those of the appropriate age and health, and homefront war jobs for those who were too old or too infirm, but women were also called upon to do their bit. While certain groups and socioeconomic classes of women have always been in the workforce, WWII brought an important societal change in that middle and upper class women also were expected to contribute to the war effort through outside-the-home employment as well as home-based efficiencies. Women were encouraged to join the women's adjunct of the various branches of the military or to take a wartime production job building and producing tanks, planes, ammunition, and other war supplies, thus freeing up a man for military service.

At the same time, very little in the way of consumer goods and luxuries was available to the general public. For example, in 1943, U.S. automobile manufacturers were prohibited from manufacturing cars for the general public, instead being required to devote their factory space and production efforts to creating needed transportation for the war. Likewise, the country endured several well-known limitations and rationing efforts, ranging from the rationing of foodstuffs (like meat, wheat, and sugar), to the complete disappearance of luxury items like silk stockings.

Although some allied countries, notably Great Britain, saw advertising campaigns urging citizens "Don't Mind Hitler. Take Your Holiday," the United States saw little to none of these kinds of efforts. Instead, American wartime advertising focused on encouraging citizens to work hard, save resources, carpool, and keep war secrets under their hats. "Use it up. Wear it out. Make it do. Or do without," became a popular wartime saying.

The net effect in 1946 was a population that had worked very hard for five years saving up money from war production jobs and combat pay with few outlets for spending it. Counting both the Great Depression and WWII, there was a cumulative fifteen years of items withstanding repair after repair, ultimately wearing out. For many Americans, a decade and a half had been spent denying themselves luxury or having it denied to them. The idea of vacations accessible to the masses felt out of reach.

This denial created a situation that economists call "pent up demand," which is, as the name implies, a release of restraint and the satisfaction of building needs. The rebounding U.S. post-war economy went through two phases, the latter of which is most important to the history of travel and travel advertising.

The first phase, which was comprised mostly of the release of pent-up demand, saw changes in the American family. Roughly nine months and five minutes after America's soldiers came marching home from war, the Baby Boom started hitting the U.S. Couples married and began families at an impressive rate, and they wanted to give these new families the life that they had been denied for a decade and a half.

First came the single family homes in the new suburbs. Many of these new suburbs were built in plats similar to those used by William Levitt in his eponymous Levittowns, in which small houses built to a limited number of floor plan options could be quickly erected and inhabited. These new houses were soon outfitted with all of the consumer goods that marked the new American dream: kitchen appliances, laundry appliances, carpeting, a new car in the garage, and a stay at home wife.

The second phase of the recovery, beginning in roughly 1950, was one of concern for marketers. Worried that the release of pent-up demand would eventually abate, marketers sought ways to entice consumers to continue to spend. And what better way to encourage spending than to induce those new parents to take those young Baby Boomers on a family vacation?

By the 1950s, America in general and Key West specifically were in a good place for a resurgence of travel. The first Baby Boomers, born in the late post-war 1940s, were just children, old enough to travel with their parents but not yet old enough to exert the influence on culture that coming "birth of the teenager" would bring. And Key West was the right combination of easy to access and delightfully rustic.

The ease of access was driven (no pun intended) by the automobile culture, which by the 1950s had reached its zenith. Cars served as means for independence, as increasing numbers of families relied (often by necessity) on a family car rather than any sort of public transportation. The increasing popularity of the suburbs meant that almost any errand, from going to work to going to the grocery, required an automobile to make the trip practical. Suddenly, hundreds of thousands of new suburban homes boasted at least one car in the driveway or garage.

Cars also served as a status symbol and the most obvious part of the of the economic boom of the 1950s. Automobile manufacturers were careful to change visible design features of their products with each production year, most notably making changes to the tail fins, grilles, and head and tail lights, all of which did not require substantial reengineering but all of which served as very noticeable markers of who was driving this year's car and who was driving an older model. In fact, automobile manufacturers actively sought the customer who would trade in a vehicle on a new model each year. The growing affluence of the country also contributed to the development of the two-car family, with one car often a "family" car able to handle the demands of young children.

Additionally, the development of the interstate highway system made longer trips by car a possibility. Most important of these to Key West was U.S. 1, a highway that began in 1911 as an auto trail called the Quebec-Miami International Highway, later named the Atlantic Highway. U.S. 1 would become the iconic North-South arterial connecting Fort Kent, Maine, with Key West. As shown in Figure 16, travel signage took advantage of interest in this unique north-south connection, welcoming travelers to Key West on one side and on the other side letting them know that their northbound journey could end at the Canadian border if they so desired.

The sign that adorned U.S. 1[85] can be seen as a statement of how Key West was relating to the country in the 1950s. It is true that Key West saw itself as connected in important ways to the mainland almost from its foundings. Certainly, by the time Flagler's railroad was in operation, travelers were making the journey from New York to Key West and on to Havana and points south, connecting the north and the south of the country.

But this sign has a different feel. This is an enticement for the family to explore the eastern seaboard, offering the potential for an adventure that spans the entire country, but in a way that is contained

Figure 16: U.S. Route 1 sign on North Roosevelt Boulevard c. 1950. (Available under Creative Commons with attribution: Florida Keys Public Library MM00004977x.)

and channeled by the highway. And, by naming Fort Kent and Key West as termini of the journey, it effectively bounds the trip to stay within the continental U.S. instead of looking north into Canada and south into the Caribbean. A companion sign at the end of U.S. 1 was even more explicit. Declaring the spot to be the "end of the rainbow and end of the route," the sign denoting the end of U.S. 1 has a very definite terminal feel, indicating clearly that the long journey south had come to an end.

In fact, by the end of the 1950s and the beginnings of the 1960s, Key West was actively courting families as visitors. In a special section touting the Florida Keys as an ideal travel destination, *The Miami Herald* sought to entice families to visit in what was still firmly located in the "off season:"[86]

> Summertime is budget time in the Florida Keys. Not only do motel and hotels reduce their rates, but they lavish extra services. Families can live it up in de luxe [sic] suites at modest rates and have a planned program of free fun thrown in on the side. Parents can have a carefree vacation while their youngsters enjoy recreation too.

The article continues to tout the traditional attractions that have sold Key West from the earliest days of tourism: "During the day, [parents] may enjoy activities ranging from golfing to yacht cruises and sightseeing expeditions. Get-together sessions, cocktail parties, and dances may be on their evening agenda."[87] However, the article goes on to emphasize family-friendly options. "Free museums and libraries may offer educational opportunities every age group can enjoy. Mom may be intrigued by a 'house of tomorrow,' while Dad and Junior view a space-age exhibit or movie."[88]

This short article, appearing in a supplement that the author of the piece and the newspaper have likely long forgotten, is a telling example of the way Key West had begun to market itself to the masses. Some eight years before Disney World would become Orlando's premiere vacation attraction, the copy from this article predicted the very aspects that Disney would capitalize on in its first years: educational opportunities and exhibits that showed the wonders of life that were (hopefully) just a few years in the future. In an approach very characteristic of the 1960s, any aspects of life that celebrated the technological advances that hit the public in the post-war era and the excitement of the on-going space race were an automatic draw for families.

However, one other aspect of this article speaks volumes about the changes taking place in the Key West travel economy. In this article, we can see the island attempting to supplement its income by attracting a different clientele during the "off season." Where once the majestic Casa Marina could make its living in the 1920s on three months of affluent travelers, sunning themselves in potentially-naked decadence during the day and donning full outfits including stockings and cloche hats for the evening, now the economy was starting to depend on the budget-conscious family to round out its yearly schedule by visiting during school vacations, even if that meant coming to the island during its very hottest months.

Rubbing Elbows

Once World War II had ended, life began to return to normal, and this includes the popular Casa Marina. Emmett Conniff, hotel manager during this period, explains the return of popularity of the resort: "It was the talk of the hotel industry. More was written about Casa Marina and its doings by nationally known columnists than all other Florida resorts combined. The place was a must with all the smart set. You just didn't rate if you hadn't paid us a visit. My phone rang many times at 3 a.m. with calls from celebrities trying to make reservations."[89]

Celebrities were obsessed with keeping up with the Joneses (or the Trumans, since Harry S Truman spent so much time in Key West), so it stands to reason that Mr. and Mrs. America shared this interest in displaying their comparative wealth. In an era in which status was communicated by the latest tail fins peeking out from the garages of "snout houses" and the most modern color of washer and dryer (that matches the stove and refrigerator, naturally), where and how one vacationed would necessarily communicate the same information. The influx of celebrities and powerful and influential people (Like Truman, John Jacob Aster, and Cornelius Vanderbilt) into the Keys meant that a trip to Key West was becoming a status symbol.

But travel to Key West in the 1950s did not necessarily mean the most luxurious of accommodations, and the Casa was not the only option. As the postcard in Figure 17[90] clearly shows, many visitors to Key West in the post-war era were happy to stay in small cottages that didn't feature beachfront property or ocean views. As has always been true of a small island like Key West, no matter where one stays, one is only a short walk from the ocean, and the prestige of

Figure 17: Postcard of the Ocean View Hotel cottages, c. 1950. (Available under Creative Commons with attribution: Florida Keys Public Library MM00013313x.)

vacationing there was easily communicated to family and friends to the north, first through such picture postcards, and second through the interminable slide reels that would be trotted out at family gatherings for some time to come after.

Vintage Selfies: The Postcard as Travel Marketing

To many modern travelers, no trip is complete without a chronicle of the trip's events posted to social media like Facebook or Instagram. Carefully constructed shots that show luxurious lodgings or exotic terrain do not only allow the traveler to share their experience with friends and family; more to the point, they deliver the implicit message, "I'm here, and you're not."

Marketers of experiences depend on this kind of messaging to sell their facilities and events to others. It is a common marketing technique. Especially when dealing with discretionary purchases, the marketing value of "keeping up with the Joneses" cannot be overestimated. While necessities – like soap, toothpaste, and even, in some circumstances, base model cars – are often sold by touting the features and benefits of the product, discretionary, or luxury, purchases are typically sold by emphasizing their role in a lifestyle that the consumer wants to attain. Often known as "aspirational" advertising, ads for such products and experiences sell the fantasy that the consumer will be part of an elevated class of consumer with the addition of that product to their lives.

For experiential luxuries, aspirational forms of advertising are particularly important. Whereas a new watch or a piece of clothing conducts its own "word of mouth" advertising every time someone wears it, a trip to an exotic locale exists only in the words and photos of the traveler. Today, that kind of word of mouth advertising often takes place on an ad hoc basis through social media, but for many decades, it was the postcard that carried the message of the lifestyle the sender was, at least temporarily, leading.

Although postcards have existed since the beginning of postal mail delivery, they arguably reached their zenith of popularity in the mid-twentieth century, particularly in the use of travel advertising. Travelers would often purchase postcards at each stop along their route, penning a cheery "wish you were here" message to friends and family, then dropping the card in a mailbox, where it would seemingly always begin a journey home so circuitous that the traveler would arrive home first.

What is so interesting about postcards, especially those advertising travel to Key West during the 1950s, is the almost understated portrayal of luxury apparent in most of them. Not every destination could be the Casa Marina; many hotels offered fairly modest accommodations, but the exotic locale and lifestyle depicted was enough to spark envy in the postcard recipient.

Take, for example, a postcard from the Sun and Sand Club[91], just a few blocks away from the Casa and clearly, from its card, offering beachfront access near the Southernmost Point. The facilities appear modest: a small pier, a row of beach chairs and umbrellas, and an unassuming building. But it is the secondary pictures that tell the real story. In the upper right, we see a tiki bar, filled with rattan furniture and offering a fully stocked bar, clearly speaking of days filled with exotic cocktails (a reputation that Key West has never shed).

Figure 18: Sun and Sand Club Postcard, 1435 Simonton Street. (Available under Creative Commons with attribution: Florida Keys Public Library MM00032654.)

In the lower right, the restaurant scene tells even more. Alone among a sea of plain white-clothed tables with straight-backed chairs, a group of tourists leans in for some interesting conversation. (One hopes that the Sun and Sand Club was somewhat more heavily booked during normal operating hours.) Most striking, however, is the diners' attire. At least one woman wears what could be either a strapless dress or, more likely, a one-piece bathing suit from the era. The message here is clear: when in Key West, the normal rules of society need not apply. The luxury of walking from hotel room to beach, dining in the most casual attire, and engaging in what would later be idiomatically called "day drinking" were already on display as an attraction of Key West, and arguably they may have been even more appealing in the somewhat more formal Fifties.

These types of postcards, which featured the property at which a traveler would stay, were ubiquitous during the period. Another example is the postcard from the Santa Maria at 1401 Simonton Street.[92]

Figure 19: Santa Maria Postcard, 1401 Simonton Street. (Available under Creative Commons with attribution: Florida Keys Public Library MM00032658.)

The card depicts a fairly standard-for-the-era single level hotel, reminiscent of the "motor hotels" or motels that were popping up along interstate highways across the country. The accommodations look comfortable and inviting, if not palatial like the Casa. What really sells the property, however, is what has sold travelers on Key West for the better part of two centuries: a picture of a cloudless bluesky punctuated by two palm trees, silent testimony to the warm weather and exotic location to be found.

A similar example is the postcard of a bird's eye view of Cactus Terrace, located at 725 Truman Avenue.[93] Yet another depiction of a vacation property, this card shows the individual cottages that made up the improbably-named Cactus Terrace. Again, the foliage makes the case: palm trees and bougainvillea dot the property, emphasizing the tropical climate that is the primary draw of this vacation spot.

One of the more interesting aspects of these property postcards is their lack of a call to action. Although copywriters would insist that most forms of advertising should have an explicit call to action, these

Figure 20: Postcard of Cactus Terrace, 725 Truman Avenue. (Available under Creative Commons with attribution: Florida Keys Public Library MM00032650.)

calls are absent from these postcards, with not a "Visit Key West" or "Stay at Cactus Terrace" in sight. In fact, the postcards for the Santa Maria and Cactus Terrace barely have any identification on their front side at all, relying only on the presence of the property sign to identify the scene.

Implicit in many of these postcards is the idea that Key West sells itself, a proposition that few who have visited the island would argue with. One such postcard[94] seemed particularly intent on letting the beauty of the island speak for itself. Showing an iconic view of the Key West Lighthouse surrounded by palm trees and other vegetation, the postcard allows the recipient to enjoy an almost-stereotypical tropical view, characterized by exotic flora and a nod to a maritime history. The caption, however, leaves much to be desired if one is looking for a reason to travel all the way to the southernmost city in the U.S.: "The Only Lighthouse in the United States Entirely Within City Limits, Key West, Florida." If one is looking for a unique selling proposition for visiting the island, it is far better that the viewer look to the palm trees rather than the location of the lighthouse.

Figure 21: A postcard of President Eisenhower on Truman Avenue. (Available under Creative Commons with attribution: Florida Keys Public Library MM00013524x.)

Finally, some postcards seem less a vehicle for advertising than they do an elaborate inside joke, as does the card in figure 21[95], which shows President Dwight Eisenhower riding in a convertible past the Margaret-Truman Launderette. Although the Launderette was doubtless named for its location at the intersection of Margaret Street and Truman Avenue instead of for the former president's daughter, the looming presence of the Margaret Truman name along with the nearby location of Truman's Little White House serve to give those in the know a chuckle about the shadow of Harry S Truman over his successor. Even the color of the building behind the matching presidential motorcade seems to suggest that this is Harry's town, and Ike will have to work to make his mark.

Jennifer Patterson Lorenzetti

CHAPTER 6: BEFORE MARGARITAVILLE
Conch and Visitor in Key West

Ask many Conchs their opinion of Jimmy Buffet, the iconic singer and songwriter whose country/Caribbean fusion music has become the accidental soundtrack for all of those who want to quit their day jobs and move to the Keys, and you will likely get some mixed responses. On the one hand, the island benefits from the tourism that Buffet brings to the island. Buffet fans, known as Parrotheads, flock to the island for an annual festival that celebrates his music. Year round, many tourists who visit the island by cruise ship can be seen walking Duval Street carrying the highly-recognizable Margaritaville carrier bag, indicating that they have made a stop at the singer/songwriter/businessman's first in a chain of restaurants and gift shops. For many, the inaugural (and perhaps subsequent) visit to the island is not complete without the chance to drink a margarita, eat a "cheeseburger in paradise," and leave with a souvenir t-shirt, all of which contribute to the influx of tourism dollars to the island.

However, one has to have some empathy for the locals. No matter whether or not they enjoy Buffet's music (and many do), it is easy to tire of hearing "Margaritaville" on frequent repeat on the soundtrack in many restaurants, to bore of hearing "Boat Drinks" played on every sunset cruise, or to be a musician continually asked to perform a cover of the singer's hit songs. The fact that many tourists associate the island more with a single artist's catalog of music than remember the rich history and wide array of artists the island has brought to the world is at least worth a gusty sigh.

But the association of the island with "Margaritaville" does not truly take hold until the last decades of the twentieth century, placing it beyond the scope of our study. Buffet himself did not arrive in Key West until the early 1970s, and it can be argued that the man whose music shaped many perceptions of the island fell in love with a Key West that would soon disappear. Indeed, his official website bio explains, "Jimmy Buffett had never before seen the Florida Keys. Key West was an outpost over 100 miles from our mainland - closer to Cuba than to Florida - a place of fascinating history and charm, dependent upon the ocean for much of its income yet subject to the whims of weather and the perils of change. Jimmy's discovery of the island meant everything to the man."[96]

Buffett was neither the first nor the last to experience an era of change driven by the need to attract visitors to the island. The 1960s and 70s brought many developments in tourism that would be familiar to visitors today, albeit in forms that were quirky and a little rough around the edges, much like the island itself.

Marketing to the Conchs

Although Key West has a long history of marketing to transient populations who would stay on the island for a short time, it is undeniable that the island has always attracted a significant group of people who come and never leave – or, at least, who visit so regularly or for so long that they become a part of the day-to-day life of the island. Yesterday's salvage industry workers became the modern first families after which streets are named; socialites who came "for the season" dedicated a quarter or more of their years to living in Key West. Even modern visitors, beyond the scope of study of this book, soon learn that a three-day long weekend in Key West is good, but a three month rental is better, often leading to the purchase of a home and a change of latitude.

What this means for the advertising for Key West is that advertising to attract people to the island often sits side by side with advertising directed to the temporary or permanent resident. And, the advertising meant for the population of Conchs and residents has a far different flavor that the romanticized portrayals of palm trees and year-round sun.

Take, for example, a 1965 guide to the island, *Louise White Shows You Key West*.[97] This charming book introduces those not familiar with the island to topics such as its history, its lodgings and restaurants, and its unique activities. The interior advertising, however, is plain and functional, reminiscent of the sort of advertising sold in support of a high school yearbook.

For example, the chapter on history includes an advertisement for the Florida First National Bank at Key West.[98] With a stylized headline, "We Remember When," the ad links back to the content on the surrounding page and employs a latter-day version of Arts and Crafts style design with a detailed reproduction of a Mario Sanchez piece surrounded by a simple border and a fair amount of body copy. It is clear, however, that the ad is directed far more to the permanent local population than to a transient visitor. "Yes, we remember the horse and buggy, the first auto and the many other milestones of yesterdays! Now we look to an even brighter tomorrow that will realize our every dream!" the copy enthuses. Not a word is mentioned about banking services for a transient population.

The advertisement for Key West State Bank on the following page perhaps does a somewhat better job identifying its target market.[99] In a text-only piece stylistically reminiscent of broadside advertisements from the late 1800s (although with a good deal more white space and restraint on use of multiple typefaces), the bank bills itself as "your hometown – homeowned bank," a clear call to the local population who might read this guide. The middle of the piece does comment on the bank's "complete correspondent service for our tourist friends," which does identify the transient visitor as a potential patron. However, it is the final line that most clearly suggests the reason the bank may be advertising in a guide to the island: "operating the only military banking facility in Monroe County."

Stylistically, ads created by local businesses are also often delightfully out of step with the prevailing advertising styles of their time. While the early 1960s brought the "Creative Revolution" to Madison Avenue advertising, exemplified by clean lines, ample white space, and a close connection between the illustration and the minimal body copy, an ad in Louise White's book for The General Store[100] would have been much more at home in the 1880s than the 1960s. Boasting no fewer than 12 fonts within a 3.5" x 4" space, along with a number of icons reminiscent of early woodcuts, the ad is nothing short of a visual cacophony. The creators of such classic 1960s ads as the VW "Think Small" piece would have been horrified.

However, there is arguably a method to the advertiser's madness (likely along with a desire to play with typography). First, the ad is for "The General Store," a business that very likely cultivated a vintage feel for its shoppers, so advertising in vintage style was a logical choice. Equally important, however, is that the ad ran in a visitor's guide that was likely perused at some leisure by vacationers and others who had more time to read. Far from a billboard on a busy highway or a street sign that one would walk quickly past, this ad appears in a context that invites time spent reading, and it invites the viewer to slow down and work his or her way through the fonts to the underlying message, just as was true in the 1800s when such ads were popular in newspapers.

Overall, the guide is just one example of the fact that much of the marketing of the island was directed not only to entice visitors to come to the island but also to acquaint those already in temporary residence to take advantage of the benefits of being there. With a robust chapter explaining the presence of the military and other listings noting churches, civic clubs, parks, and even an explanation of the then-popular hobby of "bottle digging," guides like this may have found the largest part of their audience among residents who served in the military and other populations who need to get acquainted with their new home on Cayo Hueso.

The Mallory Square Sunset Celebration

Today, no visit to Key West is considered complete without a visit to the Sunset Celebration at Mallory Square. Commencing two hours before sunset each night, the cruise ships leave their docks and a variety of vendors set up to sell their wares, ranging from handmade jewelry to art prints and food items. Street performers line the square and draw crowds, and, as of this writing, the sounds of salsa music performed by local favorite band Caribe of Key West waft from the old cigar factory that is now El Meson de Pepe, where the Cuban food is dished up hot and the mojitos are flowing.

But in the 1970s, the Sunset Celebration was not quite the tourist attraction that it is today. According to the website of the Key West Cultural Preservation Society, which manages the Sunset Celebration:

> The contemporary incarnation of Sunset Celebration really took off in the late 1960's as groups of carefree gypsies descended upon Key West and Mallory Pier in search of paradise. The way that the sunset ceremony got started is that all the "freaks," as drug users were called in the sixties, used to go down every evening high on LSD to watch Atlantis arising mythically out of the cloud formations at sunset.[101]

The site goes on to explain that, at the time, the dock included signs announcing, "no peddling on the pier," making vending operations a bit of a rebellion. Additionally, the dock was being renovated to accommodate the cruise ships that would soon become a staple of Key West tourism. Where once the sponging, turtling, and tobacco ships could directly up to the factories that line Wall Street to unload their cargo for processing, now an expansive brick square was being constructed, lined with cruise ship docks.

To control the growth of the vendor participation in the Sunset Celebration, the Key West Cultural Preservation Society was formed in 1984 to manage the celebration and act as a gateway through which artists must pass in order to sell their wares or make their performances at the nightly ritual. But, all of this was in the future as of the early 1970s, with the Celebration still a free-form gathering of all who wished to experience the beauty of a Key West sunset, which never grows old no matter how many times one experiences it.

Air Sunshine

Ask many locals of "a certain age," and they will fondly remember Air Sunshine, a small airline that flew a route encompassing Tampa, Miami, and the Keys from 1974 to 1978.[102] As the only airline serving the Keys at the time, Air Sunshine was one reason that Key West preserved some of its feeling of "otherworldliness" well into the 1970s. Although travel had become much faster than sixty years previous, when visitors would take either a ship or Flagler's new railroad, they were still limited to either traversing Flagler's land route (this time by car) or Air Sunshine.

The airline was reputedly known as "Air Sometimes" because of its tendency to rather loosely regard scheduled arrival and departure times. Local bars would reputedly announce "last flight out" rather than "last call," the signal that visitors should make their way to the airport for the 11:00 p.m. flight. If the airplane's crew happened to be visiting the local watering holes, there was every chance that the "last flight out" would not occur until the next morning, but this was of little consequence. Key West has always been notoriously difficult to leave.

According to one account,[103] even the airport staff at other airports would treat "Air Sometimes" passengers a little more casually than those for other airlines. In one conversation this author had with a Key West resident reminiscing about air travel to the island in the 1970s, the announcements for flights leaving Miami could speak volumes about the casual nature of Key West. According to the traveler, after formally announcing the departure of certain flights, all properly identified by flight number and final destination, the airport staff member would look around the remaining travelers, all waiting for Air Sunshine, and simply announce, "Key West, load 'em up!"

Jennifer Patterson Lorenzetti

EPILOGUE
"Wonder why we ever go home"[104]

    Not so long ago, some visitors to Key West would step off a train onto the dusty depot platform, tired from their travels, headed for the comforts of a hotel before continuing on their journey south. Having grown accustomed over the last couple of hundred miles to increasingly warm temperatures, they were no doubt ready for a change of clothes and a rest from the bumpy ride that the railroad inevitably would provide.

    Today, many visitors arrive by plane. The small regional jet makes its descent into Key West and lands precipitously, the pilot slamming on the brakes and the passengers bracing themselves against the seat in front of them, propelled by the forces resulting from an effort to land on the necessarily-short runway. Experienced visitors will sometimes declare, "that wasn't too bad!" to herald a pilot who can perform this task with only a few bumps and jolts. Soon, the plane taxis up to the tarmac outside the arrivals gate at the small airport.

    Most days out of the year, the heat and humidity strike all at once as one deplanes and descends the portable stairs wheeled up to facilitate exit; there is no collapsible walkway here. Instead, tourists feel the sun on their skin immediately, become wrapped in the heavy air, and smell the salty-fishy scent of the ocean as they descend to the tarmac and head for the airport. On the way, they will take a look at (and sometimes a photo of) the delightfully kitschy statue of several wholesome-looking people gesturing happily to a replica of the Southernmost Point marker, with "Welcome to Key West" in Art Deco lettering below. In much larger lettering, signage above the second floor windows of the airport proclaims, "Welcome to the Conch Republic."

Once inside the airport, the advertising begins immediately. Digital signage above the baggage claim conveyor advertises bars and shopping opportunities, and tourists will take out their phones to photograph coupon codes good for discounts, drink specials, or free appetizers with purchase. They may even take advantage of the new (as of this writing) First Call bar, where they can start the party before even being reunited with their suitcases.

The advertising will continue throughout the visit. Every taxi driver, restaurant owner, and hotel concierge will have a complementary map to pass out, framed with paid ads for local attractions, while a tight referral network ensures that the taxi driver will pass out a coupon for a local restaurant, at which the server will recommend the best ice cream place, at which the cashier will give instructions as to how to book a jet ski tour, on which the tour guide will recommend a favorite bar. And on and on it goes.

Step off Duval Street, however, and the atmosphere starts to change. Those who worry that old Key West has disappeared have a valid argument, but one can see its echoes in the Victorian architecture and the little-known locals' spots that are whispered about rather than shouted of from digital signage. Conversations, too, are carefully gauged. The same waitress or cab driver who offers up the standard small talk of "where are you from?" and "what's the weather like back home?" will soon start sharing favorite hidden spots upon learning that this is not a first (or fifth, or tenth) visit to the island. Pretty soon, the conversation turns to "what's your favorite month here?" and "when are you moving down?" The locals are nothing if not enthusiastic about sharing their love of the island and the story of how they came to Cayo Hueso, whether that was as recently as a retirement move or as far back as a family move during the founding years.

Key West has always been an island that must be taken on its own terms. Oppressive heat, hurricanes, and rocky beaches on a coral reef balance out the sub-tropical, frost-free climate, the palm trees, and the ocean views that are never more than a few minutes' walk away. Those who cannot love this harsh but vibrant mix can always find the last flight out ready to take them back to their place of origin. But for those who truly love her, Key West will always be a magical place that defies any slick advertising that could ever be produced.

Jennifer Patterson Lorenzetti

Prologue

[1] Jimmy Buffett, *Fruitcakes*, Fruitcakes, © 1994 by Margaritaville Records/MCA, MCAD-11043, CD.

[2] Dineen, Caitlin. "Florida welcomed nearly 113 million tourists in 2016." *Orlando Sentinel*, February 16, 2017. Accessed May 26, 2017. http://www.orlandosentinel.com/travel/os-bz-visit-florida-tourism-2016-story.html.

[3] Standiford, Les. *Last train to paradise: Henry Flagler and the spectacular rise and fall of the railroad that crossed an ocean.* (New York: Three Rivers Press, 2002) 197.

Chapter 1

[4] Bramson, Seth. *The greatest railroad story ever told: Henry Flagler & the Florida East Coast Railway's Key West extension.* (Charleston, S.C.: History Press, 2011), 22-23.

[5] Bramson, Seth. *The greatest railroad story ever told: Henry Flagler & the Florida East Coast Railway's Key West extension.* (Charleston, S.C.: History Press, 2011), 30.

[6] Bramson, Seth. *The greatest railroad story ever told: Henry Flagler & the Florida East Coast Railway's Key West extension.* (Charleston, S.C.: History Press, 2011), 33.

[7] Bramson, Seth. *The greatest railroad story ever told: Henry Flagler & the Florida East Coast Railway's Key West extension.* (Charleston, S.C.: History Press, 2011), 39.

[8] Bramson, Seth. *The greatest railroad story ever told: Henry Flagler & the Florida East Coast Railway's Key West extension.* (Charleston, S.C.: History Press, 2011), 42.

[9] Campbell's Soup, Advertisement, 1914.

[10] Florida East Coast Railway, Brochure, 1913. (Available under Wikimedia Commons)

[11] Florida East Coast Railway, Brochure, ca. 1920. (Courtesy Florida Keys Public Library)

[12] Key West & Monroe County, Florida, Brochure, ca. 1920. (Available under Creative Commons with attribution: Florida Keys Public Library MM00030988)

[13] Sivulka, Juliann. *Soap, sex, and cigarettes: a cultural history of American advertising*. 2nd ed. (Australia: Wadsworth, Cengage Learning, 2012), 104.

[14] Florida East Coast Railway, Brochure, ca. 1912. (Available under Creative Commons with attribution: Florida Keys Public Library MM00030826)

Chapter 2

[15] Over Sea Hotel Post Card, ca. 1915-1920. (Available under Creative Commons with attribution: De Wolfe and Wood Collection, Florida Keys Public Library MM0003032x)

[16] Over Sea Hotel Post Card, author's collection.

[17] CPI Inflation Calculator. Bureau of Labor Statistics. Retrieved May 4, 2017.

[18] The Casa Marina: Historic House by the Sea. (Key West, FL: Scarma Bay Pub., 1992), p. 14.

[19] Ibid.

[20] The Casa Marina: Historic House by the Sea. (Key West, FL: Scarma Bay Pub., 1992), p. 16.

[21] Ibid

[22] Sivulka, Juliann. *Soap, sex, and cigarettes: a cultural history of American advertising*. 2nd ed. (Australia: Wadsworth, Cengage Learning, 2012), p. 158.

[23] The Casa Marina: Historic House by the Sea. (Key West, FL: Scarma Bay Pub.,

1992), p. 23.

[24]Ibid

[25]Ibid.

[26] Signage, Casa Marina, Key West Art and Historical Society display. From the collection of the author.

[27] Ibid.

[28] CPI Inflation Calculator. Bureau of Labor Statistics. Retrieved September 15, 2016.

[29] Flagler Hotel Artifacts from The Bramson Archive. Key West Art and Historical Society display. From the author's collection.

[30] "Interview with Tom Hambright." Interview by author. November 29, 2016.

[31]The Casa Marina: Historic House by the Sea. (Key West, FL: Scarma Bay Pub., 1992), p. 26.

[32] Kerstein, Robert J. Key West on the edge: inventing the Conch Republic. (Gainesville: University Press of Florida, 2012), p. 41.

[33] Hemingway, E.M., To Have and Have Not.

[34] Kerstein, Robert J. Key West on the edge: inventing the Conch Republic. (Gainesville: University Press of Florida, 2012), p. 40.

[35] Kerstein, Robert J. Key West on the edge: inventing the Conch Republic. (Gainesville: University Press of Florida, 2012), p. 34.

[36] Kerstein, Robert J. Key West on the edge: inventing the Conch Republic. (Gainesville: University Press of Florida, 2012), p. 34-35.

[37] Sivulka, Juliann. *Soap, sex, and cigarettes: a cultural history of American advertising*. 2nd ed. (Australia: Wadsworth, Cengage Learning, 2012), p. 110-113.

[38] "The Penalty of Leadership." Library of Congress. Retrieved September 8,

2016.

[39] Sivulka, Juliann. *Soap, sex, and cigarettes: a cultural history of American advertising*. 2nd ed. (Australia: Wadsworth, Cengage Learning, 2012), p. 104-108.

[40] Ibid.

[41] Google Books Ngram Viewer search. Retrieved October 19, 2016.

[42] http://panam.org/take-off/555-first-flight-oct-19-1928. Retrieved September 8, 2016.

[43] http://www.atlasobscura.com/places/pan-am-s-first-office Retrieved September 8, 2016.

[44] The Casa Marina: Historic House by the Sea. (Key West, FL: Scarma Bay Pub., 1992), p. 26.

[45] Ibid.

Chapter 3

[46] Brochure pages from the Otto Hirzel scrapbook about Key West, ca. late 1930s-late 1940s. (Available under Creative Commons with attribution: Florida Keys Public Library MM41339-47x)

[47] Key West guide book; an aid to the visitor - Fall and Winter, 1935-1936. Key West Administration, 1935.

[48] Kerstein, Robert J. *Key West on the edge: inventing the Conch Republic.* (Gainesville: University Press of Florida, 2012), p. 48.

[49] 907 Whitehead Street photo from the Scott DeWolfe Collection from the Florida Keys Public Library. (Available under Creative Commons with attribution: Florida Keys Public Library MM00042282x)

[50] Hemingway, E.M., *To Have and Have Not*.

[51] Kerstein, Robert J. *Key West on the edge: inventing the Conch Republic.* (Gainesville: University Press of Florida, 2012), p. 58.

[52] Key West Aquarium tour, author.

[53] Key West Aquarium ca. 1950. (Available under Creative Commons with attribution: Florida Keys Public Library MM00039510x)

[54] Key West Aquarium Construction photo from the Florida Keys Public Library. (Available under Creative Commons with attribution: Florida Keys Public Library MM00033834x)

[55] "The Aquarium Frescoes," Signage, The Key West Aquarium. Referenced from photo from author's collection.

[56] Ibid.

[57] Writers' Program of the Works Progress Administration in the State of Florida, comp. A Guide to Key West. New York: Hastings House, 1949.

[58] Ibid.

[59] Ibid.

[60] Ibid.

[61] Ibid.

[62] Hollowell, Maude Haynes, ed. Go to Sea Key West: Gibraltar of America. December 1939.

[63] Ibid.

[64] Kerstein, Robert J. Key West on the edge: inventing the Conch Republic. (Gainesville: University Press of Florida, 2012), p. 46-47.

[65] McIver, Stuart B. Hemingway's Key West. Sarasota, FL: Pineapple Press, 2002.

[66] Hemingway, Ernest. "Who Murdered the Vets?" The New Masses, September 17, 1935, 9-10.

[67] Ibid.

[68] Chevrolet Leader News, Vol. 1, No. 2, 1935. Accessed from YouTube June 29, 2015 under Creative Commons License.

[69] Brochure pages from the Otto Hirzel scrapbook about Key West, ca. late 1930s-late 1940s. (Available under Creative Commons with attribution: Florida Keys Public Library MM41339-13x)

Chapter 4

[70] Signage, "Why Key West," Key West Art and Historical Society display. From the photo collection of the author.

[71] Ibid.

[lxxii] Illustration plate from *Harper's Weekly*, April 18, 1874. From the Monroe County Library Collection. (Available under Creative Commons with attribution: Florida Keys Public Library MM00041084x)

[73] Signage, Key West Art and Historical Society, viewed November 30, 2017. Author's collection.

[74] Ibid.

[75] The Casa Marina: Historic House by the Sea. (Key West, FL: Scarma Bay Pub., 1992), p. 28.

[76] Ibid.

[77] Kerstein, Robert J. Key West on the edge: inventing the Conch Republic. (Gainesville: University Press of Florida, 2012), p. 61-62.

[78] Ibid.

[79] "Key West Visits," Harry S. Truman Little White House web site (www.trumanlittlewhitehouse.com). Accessed on 9 March, 2017.

[80] "Military History of Key West" Harry S. Truman Little White House web site (www.trumanlittlewhitehouse.com). Accessed on 9 March, 2017.

[81] Kerstein, Robert J. Key West on the edge: inventing the Conch Republic. (Gainesville: University Press of Florida, 2012), p. 81

[82] Ibid.

[83] Kerstein, Robert J. Key West on the edge: inventing the Conch Republic. (Gainesville: University Press of Florida, 2012), p. 99.

[84] Ibid.

Chapter 5

[85] U.S. Route 1 sign on North Roosevelt Boulevard c. 1950. (Available under Creative Commons with attribution: Florida Keys Public Library MM00004977x.)

[86] "A Few Words for the Budgeteers." The Miami Herald (Miami), January 13, 1963, The Golden Lure of the Florida Keys sec. Supplemental Section.

[87] Ibid.

[88] Ibid.

[89] The Casa Marina: Historic House by the Sea. (Key West, FL: Scarma Bay Pub., 1992), p. 30.

[90] Ocean View Hotel Postcards, c. 1950. (Available under Creative Commons with attribution: Florida Keys Public Library MM00013313x.)

[91] Sun and Sand Club Postcard, 1435 Simonton Street. (Available under Creative Commons with attribution: Florida Keys Public Library MM00032654.)

[92] Santa Maria Postcard, 1401 Simonton Street. (Available under Creative Commons with attribution: Florida Keys Public Library MM00032658.)

[93] Postcard of Cactus Terrace, 725 Truman Avenue. (Available under Creative Commons with attribution: Florida Keys Public Library MM00032650.)

[94] Hollis, Tim. Selling the Sunshine State: a celebration of Florida tourism advertising. (Gainesville: University Press of Florida, 2008). p. 326-327.

[95] Postcard of President Eisenhower on Truman Avenue. (Available under Creative Commons with attribution: Florida Keys Public Library MM00013524x.)

Chapter 6

[96] "Jimmy in Key West." Margaritaville Key West website. http://www.margaritavillekeywest.com/jb-in-keywest.html Retrieved 10 November, 2016.

[97] White, Louise V. Louise White shows you Key West; a guide to an enchanting city. St. Petersburg, FL: Great Outdoors Pub. Co., 1965.

[98] Ibid.

[99] Ibid.

[100] Ibid.

[101] "History of Sunset Celebration, Key West Cultural Preservation Society Website. http://www.sunsetcelebration.org/history.htm Retrieved 17 November, 2016.

[102] "Air Sunshine." Sunshine Skies Website. http://www.sunshineskies.com/airsunshine.html Retrieved 10 November, 2016.

[103] Airplane traveler, personal communication with author, ca. 2010.

Epilogue

[104] Jimmy Buffett, Wonder Why We Ever Go Home, Changes in Latitudes, Changes in Attitudes, © 1977 by ABC Records.

ABOUT THE AUTHOR

Jennifer Patterson Lorenzetti is an experienced writer and educator with a deep love of all things Key West. She has taught at the college level for over a decade, including designing and teaching History of Advertising in America. She is the author of over 1600 published articles and copywriting projects completed through her writing and speaking firm, Hilltop Communications, as well as four other published books.

Learn more at www.hilltopcommunications.net, or contact her at lorenzetti.jennifer@hilltopcommunications.net

www.ingramcontent.com/pod-product-compliance
Lightning Source LLC
Chambersburg PA
CBHW042323150426
43192CB00001B/26